M000268273

Ribera

Michael Scholz-Hänsel

Jusepe de
Ribera

1591–1652

KÖNEMANN

Frontispiece
1 Drunken Silenus (detail of ill. 87)

© 2000 Könemann Verlagsgesellschaft mbH
Bonner Strasse 126, D-50968 Cologne

Publishing and Art Direction: Peter Feierabend
Project Management: Ute Edda Hammer, Jeannette Fentroß
Editing: Bärbel Reyners-Krupp, Dossenheim
Layout: Andrea Mehlhose & Martin Wellner, Cologne
Picture Research: Stefanie Huber
Lithography: Digiprint, Erfurt

Original title: *Meister der spanischen Kunst. Jusepe de Ribera*

© 2000 for this English edition:
Könemann Verlagsgesellschaft mbH

Translation from German: Paul Aston in association with Cambridge Publishing Management
Editing: Sally Simmons in association with Cambridge Publishing Management
Typesetting: Cambridge Publishing Management
Project Management: Jackie Dobbyne for Cambridge Publishing Management, Cambridge, UK
Project Coordination: Kristin Zeier
Production: Oliver Benecke
Printing and Binding: Neue Stalling, Oldenburg
Printed in Germany

ISBN 3-8290-2872-5

10 9 8 7 6 5 4 3 2 1

Contents

NEITHER SPANISH NOR ITALIAN

2 *Allegory of Touch*, c. 1613
Oil on canvas, 114 x 88 cm
Norton Simon Foundation, Pasadena

What could better illustrate the sense of touch than the searching hand of a blind man? Yet Ribera goes one step further to involve another layer of meaning. While his figure, whose dress and face recall the portrait of a contemporary philosopher, feels his way round a sculptural head of antiquity, a flat picture lies on the table whose delights must remain unseen to the blind man. Possibly this is also a reference to the *paragone*, or rivalry between the arts, which in Italy had rather different connotations than it did in Spain. On the Iberian Peninsula, sculptors had long been paid far better than painters.

In 1992 a major retrospective exhibition of the works of Jusepe de Ribera visited Madrid, Naples and New York. The exhibition made clear not only how hugely knowledge about Ribera's oeuvre has advanced in recent decades but also how much still remains to be discovered. There are still amazing gaps in Ribera's biography, and important pictures still lack conclusive or convincing interpretations.

The painter was baptized on February 17, 1591 in Játiva, a town near Valencia. The baptismal document names him as Joan Josep Ribera. Later, his name and the spelling of his Christian name vary depending on the source of the document. Common forms include Giuseppe, Gioseppe and Jusepe. He himself signed his pictures Jusepe de Ribera, and this has therefore become the accepted version of his name. Several of his pictures he signed with the additional cognomen *español* or its Latin equivalent *Hispanus* (the Spaniard), or the alternative Latin terms *Valentinus* (the Valencian) or *Setabensis* (the Játivan). At a fairly early date, he also acquired the Italian nickname of *Lo Spagnoletto* (the Little Spaniard).

Jusepe de Ribera is first documented in Italy in 1611. From 1613 he was living in Rome, and from 1616 he lived in Naples. In the mid-1640s, illness began to hamper his artistic activities. After a brief recovery between 1647 and 1649, his condition once again began to worsen steadily. He died in Naples on September 3, 1652.

In art history, where the nationality of an artist always plays a key role in stylistic classifications, it is still a matter of controversy as to whether Ribera should be considered Spanish or Italian. Arguments in favor of the Italian school are that none of the works he did in Spain has so far been found, that he adopted many of the technical and stylistic innovations of Italian painters and most especially that, contrary to Spanish practice, he drew a lot. In favor of a Spanish classification are the facts that the majority of his clients and collectors came from Spain, and that his naturalism and iconography put him closer to his fellow countryman Diego Velázquez (1599–1660) than, for example, Italian contemporaries like the Bolognese painter Guido Reni, (1575–1642) or the Neapolitan Massimo Stanzione (c. 1585–1656).

The most recent attempt to claim Ribera for the Italian school was undertaken by Ronald Cohen, who represents him not only as the descendant of a noble family but also moves his birthplace to southern Italy. Newer, less well-known information indicates that this hypothesis is way off the mark, besides conflicting with the artist's own signature.

Even if all other recent publications superficially renounce a national perspective, it nonetheless persists in more subtle ways. The dispute as to how far his artistic output reflects Ribera the man, which flared up following the discovery of new pictures, merely continues the argument in a different way. It is still considered a characteristic difference between Spanish and Italian artists that the former were more closely orientated to the model of nature, while the latter reflected their own artistry, form and content theoretically as well.

Yet 17th-century Italy and Spain cannot be described with modern classifications. Today's Italy did not even exist at the time. Politically it was a highly heterogeneous entity made up of many small states, a considerable proportion of which were under Spanish rule or at least indirectly dependent on Spain. Spain, on the other hand, was referred to as *los reinos de España*, the realms of Spain or the Hispanic world, which at this period had reached its greatest extent. It meant a national territory that included not only the Iberian Peninsula but also the Netherlands and extensive holdings overseas and in Italy. Naples was ruled by a Spanish viceroy, but had a special status in that the Spanish Inquisition had no authority there. The region, placed between the Spanish world and the Church state, was thus well-placed to develop as a center of innovation. To the Spanish Habsburgs, however, it appeared to be a territory continually threatening secession.

The viceroys who were Ribera's most important patrons were accordingly kept under strict control and generally remained in office only a few years. At the time, Naples' population was far larger than that of Madrid or Barcelona, largely because of constant immigration from the countryside. In this respect, Naples was in European terms second only to Paris, and ahead of Rome. Such a large population compressed into a small space led to powerful social

4 Léon Bonnat (1833–1922)
Martyrdom of St. Philip (after Ribera), 1864
Oil on canvas, stuck on wood, 28 x 29 cm
Musée Bonnat, Bayonne

Léon Bonnat was a great admirer of Ribera, both as a painter and a collector. In his endeavors to create a realistic style in religious painting, he took the Neapolitan painter as his inspiration. When in Madrid in 1864, he copied Ribera's *Martyrdom of St. Philip* (ill. 3). In Bonnat's collection of art, now preserved in his native city of Bayonne, there are several drawings and a painting by the Spanish master.

3 (facing page)
Martyrdom of St. Philip, 1639
Oil on canvas, 234 x 234 cm
Museo del Prado, Madrid

The fact that this picture was long thought to be a representation of St. Bartholomew indicates how closely Ribera's art was identified with the martyrdom of the latter. Admittedly, a correct identification was rendered difficult in this case by the unconventional iconography, as Ribera shows not the martyrdom itself but the preparations for it. However, Ribera went about his subject in a manner typical of him, in preferring the dramatic moment before the horrible event, as he also did in the *Martyrdom of St. Bartholomew* (ill. 32). The emphasis on this drama before the martyrdom explains why the martyred saint is shown without the usual heavenly compensation for earthly suffering usual with this type of picture.

tensions, which found their most dangerous release in the Masaniello uprising of 1647/48, so named after a leader of the revolt. During the uprising, several nobles loyal to Spain were murdered, but secession from the Spanish world was prevented once again, as a result of the intervention of the Spanish military leader Don Juan José de Austria.

Although Ribera had to seek refuge in the viceregal palace at the time, up until then he had rather valued his position between the two cultures. This much is clear from a conversation recorded in 1625 in a manuscript entitled *Discursos practicables del nobilíssimo arte de la pintura* by the Spanish art writer Jusepe Martínez (1602–1682), after visiting Ribera in his Neapolitan residence. Ribera showed his fellow countryman various grand rooms and galleries in sundry large palaces, and afterwards Martinez compared his observations with his impressions of Rome, still fresh in his memory: "... everything seemed small to me, because in this city warfare and chivalry are more highly valued than artistic things; I said as much to my friend and he admitted it." When asked why such a famous artist as he didn't return to Spain, Ribera replied: "Dear friend, it would be my fervent wish, but the experience of many other sensible and honest people prevents me. Even if I were greeted as a great painter in the first year, by the second no-one would be interested in me because, if someone is there in person, he loses all respect." "I agreed with this," writes Martínez, "because I had to admit to having myself seen works by outstanding Spanish masters that were held of little account. In my judgment therefore Spain is a kindly mother to foreigners and a wicked stepmother to her own children."

By settling in Naples, Ribera was opting for an important port whose political and economic situation enabled him to be in touch with half the known world, but especially the Hispanic world. Even if the Spaniards chose to undervalue their artists compared with Italian artists in Rome and Venice, the painter found important patrons not only in southern Italy and the Iberian Peninsula but also in the Netherlands and cities like Florence and Genoa, which maintained a special relationship with the Spanish court.

In his pictures, the artist not only condensed his own experiences of a society inflamed by ecclesiastical schism and nascent globalization but also incorporated interesting moral concepts. To do this, he employed a "naturalistic" style which he stuck to all his life, even if he considerably modified it from the 1630s (ill. 2). The style is based upon an analysis of reality closely parallel to the new natural sciences founded by Galileo Galilei (1564–1642). Like the famous scientist, the artist also overcame tradition by the close observation of nature and came up with a new interpretation of reality.

The major Ribera retrospective of 1992 had weighty support from Spanish museums and private collectors. Although all Ribera's known works were created in what is now Italy, many of the artist's important works are today to be found in the Iberian Peninsula. The exhibition was almost the last in a series organized by the Museo del Prado in Madrid, presenting the leading Spanish masters of the 17th century. This relatively late appreciation of the artist is not due to his lesser importance. Scholars have been at a disadvantage because of Ribera's position between Spanish and Italian cultures and the enormously widespread distribution of his

works. Although Ribera's oeuvre continuously fascinated both his contemporaries and subsequent generations, more intensive theoretical and artistic debate only got under way in the early 19th century.

Both Jean-François Millet (1814–1875) and Henri Matisse (1869–1954) painted pictures of their own from models by the Játiva master. However, it was mainly the French painters Léon Bonnat (1833–1922) and Théodule Ribot (1823–1891) who developed into real specialists in handling the figures and atmosphere in the manner so typical of the earlier Ribera (ills. 4, 6).

The enthusiasm of 19th-century French painters for Ribera's art would have still been inconceivable in the time of Francisco de Goya (1746–1828). The few Spanish masters known at all at that time were seen as one-offs, who had made their way in opposition to national ignorance and had drawn their inspiration not from bilateral or successive dialog with other Spanish painters, but from Dutch and Italian models.

The concept of a separate "Spanish School" first developed with the institution of a Spanish Gallery by the citizen king Louis Philippe in Paris, though it lasted only ten years (1838–1848). The Spanish quality particularly singled out and esteemed was an extreme "naturalism." But the idiosyncratic treatment of saints, in which a figure such as St. Jerome appears as an emaciated hermit or the apostle Bartholomew is shown as a fearless victim of the most hideous torture, at once irritated and fascinated the viewer. Both the style and the subject matter are particularly typical of Ribera's oeuvre.

The problem of why Spanish art remained so long undiscovered takes us back to the reign of Philip II. Though Philip's patronage was instrumental in getting a "Spanish school" of Baroque painting established in the first place, he tried to stop it from communicating with the outside world. Philip's rigid isolationist policy, introduced to fend off the Reformation and Calvinism, meant not only that many artists steered clear of the Hispanic world for fear of the Inquisition but also that Spanish artists had few opportunities to travel abroad. Relying on his own greatness – Spain was the leading European power until 1640 – the king seriously underestimated the growing importance of printed graphics for the dissemination of political and artistic statements. Thus the works of Spanish artists were hardly ever made available to a larger public by means of printing in the way that had become the norm in Italy and Germany, for example.

Spanish art of the *Siglo de Oro* or Golden Age was little known outside Spain right down to the 19th century, although the geographical extent and multiple cultures of the territories ruled from Madrid achieved astonishing things. There was a constant flow of artists who were less affected by Spanish isolationism. This was particularly the case in the maritime cities that were so important for the Hispanic world as a whole and where a more liberal climate prevailed for economic reasons alone. Here, cultural interchange became the order of the day, particularly with regard

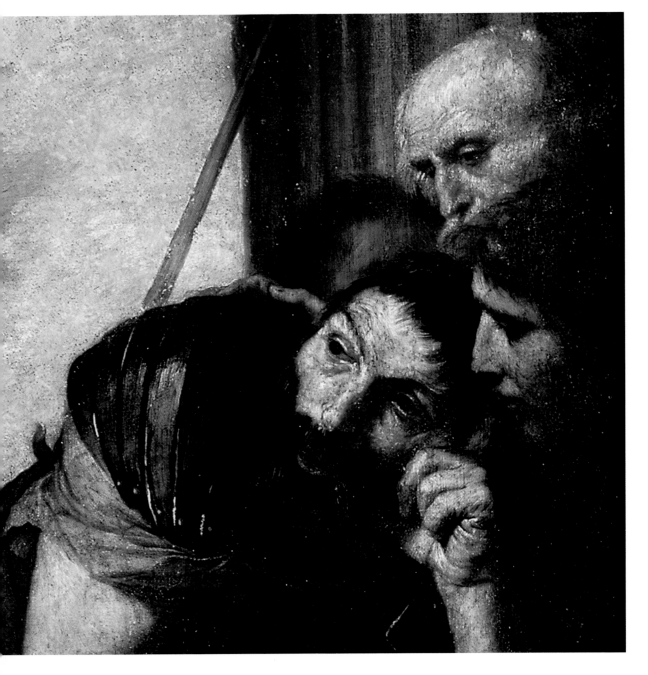

5 *Martyrdom of St. Philip* (detail of ill. 3)

Among the characteristic features of Ribera's art is the presence of witnesses at many of his scenes of martyrdom. They are individual heads, distinguished not just by the hair on their heads and faces, but also in their gestures and physiognomies, so as to suggest a unique character for each. They reveal the artist's respect for his fellow human beings, and perhaps also mirror his own role as an attentive observer of his time.

to Protestant and Calvinist countries. Among those to take advantage of it were Bartolomé Esteban Murillo (1618–1682) in Seville and Ribera in Naples. Important pictures by both artists found their way into several art collections outside Spanish-ruled territory even in the 17th century. In the Hispanic world, which in its diversity anticipated modern Europe in many respects, the painter from Játiva moved around as a kind of artistic nomad. Against the complex background of the 17th-century social and political situation, Ribera became an artistic personality whose importance extended beyond geographical frontiers. In this respect he could be considered neither Spanish nor Italian.

6 Théodule Ribot (1823–1891)
The Torture of Alonso Cano, 1867
Oil on canvas, 150 x 209 cm
Musée des Beaux-Arts, Rouen

The painter Théodule Ribot possibly became first acquainted with the works of Ribera in the Galerie Espagnole, opened by the French citizen king Louis Philippe in 1838. Ribot adopted the Spanish painter's subject matter as his own and used a similar technique. However, in contrast to Ribera he preferred tones of grey and black, in keeping with the conception of Spanish painting in his day. In its choice of subject the *Torture of Alonso Cano*, which he painted for the official Paris Salon of 1867, reflects the classic cliché of the torturing Spanish Inquisition. It is documented, however, that the celebrated artist Cano did indeed undergo a "thorough interrogation" because he was suspected of murdering his wife.

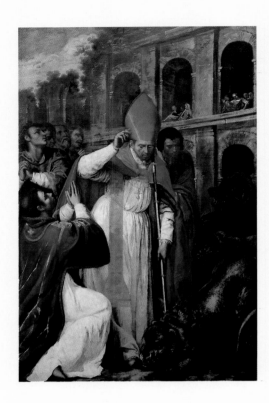

7 Artemisia Gentileschi
St. Januarius in the Amphitheater, 1637/38
Oil on canvas, 309 x 202 cm
Cathedral, Pozzuoli (deposited in the Museo Nazionale di
San Martino, Naples)

Gentileschi's decision to go to Naples was possibly
connected with the sale of several of her pictures to the
Duke of Alcalá, one of Ribera's most important patrons.
The artist was proud of her ability to paint her subjects
without a model, but she did also paint from models and
used earthy colors like Caravaggio. She was thus easily able
to blend into the Neapolitan art scene, where she also
obtained commissions from ecclesiastical institutions,
as with this picture of St. Januarius, the patron saint
of Naples.

8 (facing page)
Anthony van Dyck
Susanna Bathing, 1621/22
Oil on canvas, 194 x 144 cm
Alte Pinakothek, Bayerische Staatsgemäldesammlungen,
Munich

Gaspar Roomer was not just a collector but also dealt in
art, sending to the southern Netherlands for Flemish
paintings to exchange for Italian works. However, he
probably obtained his paintings by van Dyck on the spot,
which underlines the early success of this artist. The latter's
enthusiasm for the colors of the Venetians recurs in the
later work of Ribera. On his long journey through Italy
(1621–1627), van Dyck reached Palermo but never
visited Naples.

In 1634, a book called *Il Forasterio* was published in
Naples. It contains a detailed history and contemporary
description of the city. The author was Giulio Cesare
Capaccio (c. 1550–1631/1634) who, as secretary of the
city administration for many years, was very familiar with
the characteristics of the metropolis, and enthused over it
in sentences such as "Naples is the whole world" and
"Everyone who sees Naples wishes to die here." Over the
centuries, the city thus described so rapturously had seen a
wide range of rulers and had been exposed to a great
variety of cultural influences. The Greeks founded the first
settlement, called Parthènope, in the 8th century B.C., the
name later being revived in scholarly circles. In the 5th
century B.C. a new city or Neapolis grew up, which in 326
B.C. came under Roman control. Roman supremacy was
succeeded by Byzantine, Norman and Hohenstaufen rule.
Before the arrival of the first Spanish viceroy in 1504, the
city had also been ruled by the royal houses of Anjou
and Aragón.

Naples, to which Capaccio gave a new identity with his
book, was nonetheless more than the sum of these over-
lordships, because the 16th century brought another
important change. In the early Middle Ages, the town of
Amalfi south of Naples had served as a major trading
center between the Christian and Muslim parts of the
Mediterranean. During the subsequent military conflicts,
Amalfi, like other cities in southern Italy, lost its role as an
economic center. Trade in goods and money moved to
northern Italian cities which, led by Genoa, acquired
notable power as centers of finance. This situation
continued into the Spanish period, but there was a degree
of economic recovery in the 16th century because the
expanding metropolises of the north covered their grain
requirements from southern exports. During this period,
Naples gradually built up a key role as an entrepôt for
various goods. The population grew enormously, with
many merchants among the new arrivals. It is therefore no
mere chance that Capaccio devotes a comprehensive
section of his book to describing the districts occupied by
the different nationalities. For comparison he took ports
such as Amsterdam, Seville and Lisbon, which were structured in a similarly multi-cultural way. The term other
"nations" included Greeks as well as people from more
distant parts of Italy such as Venetians and Lombards.

If the inhabitants of Naples were more open to
foreigners than other places in Ribera's time, there were
two reasons for it, namely the vicissitudes of their own
history since Greek antiquity, and the huge change in
population structure that came with the 16th century.
Traces of the changes that were going on can be observed
not only in everyday life, but also in the artistic sphere.

Thus the Neapolitan mentality of the 17th century
encompassed both the strict etiquette of the Spanish and
an individual sense of humor imported with the many
peasant immigrants. The changed circumstances even

affected eating habits: whereas vegetables had long occupied the dominant role in the cuisine, Neapolitans now
preferred noodles, or in the words of historian Giuseppe
Galasso, they "changed from leaf- to macaroni-eaters,"
which was clearly a reaction to the ready availability of
cheap wheat.

In terms of painting, the new currents were felt in two
ways. A direct influence on the art scene was exercised by
incoming artists who settled temporarily or permanently in
the city. The first high points were two short visits by
Caravaggio in 1606/07 and 1609/10. Subsequently, besides Ribera, there were Roman artists called in to decorate
the Capella di San Gennaro in the 1630s.

The unaccustomed success of a woman painter in
Naples, Artemisia Gentileschi (1593–1652/53), becomes
comprehensible only in the context of a certain openness
(ill. 7). Born in Rome, Gentileschi came to Naples in 1630,
remaining there to the end of her days except for a brief
period in the service of Charles I in London.

The second channel by which new artistic influences
reached Naples was the art collections, which covered a
broad range as a result of the wide spectrum of trade
contacts. Along with the various Italian schools, painters
from the Netherlands were also featured prominently – as
the southern Netherlands, likewise, belonged to the
Hispanic world.

Among the artists who possibly noted Ribera's presence
were the Bamboccianti. These were a group of painters
associated with Pieter van Laer (baptized 1599-post 1642),
who lived in Rome from 1625 and was called Il Bamboccio
(The Squirt) by Italians because of his diminutive stature
(ill. 9). In their genre paintings, the Bamboccianti showed
the life of the poorer people from a crude, naturalistic
perspective, bringing the ire of classical painters down on
their heads in so doing.

Important Flemish artistic personalities in this connection also include Peter Paul Rubens and Anthony van Dyck,
whom the Flemish merchant Gaspar Roomer made
famous in Naples. He possessed Rubens' *Herod's Feast* and
a *St. Sebastian* by van Dyck along with a scene of *Susanna
Bathing* (ill. 8).

Unfortunately, the economic recovery of southern Italy
in the 16th century was only short-lived, and development
appears to have come to a halt during Ribera's day. One of
the most important reasons must be sought in the Thirty
Years' War, which tied up enormous quantities of money
that were therefore extracted from the economy. The
Madrid government attempted to cover its costs by
imposing ever more punitive taxes.

What had previously been so beneficial to Naples,
namely the influx of so many outsiders, must have heightened tensions in the new political situation. In Naples there
was the aggravating circumstance that the social discipline
which normally accompanied "confessionalization" had not
taken root to the same extent as it had in other European

9 Pieter van Laer
Landscape with Dice Players
Oil on wood, 30 x 41 cm
Alte Pinakothek, Bayerische Staatsgemäldesammlungen,
Munich

There are grounds for supposing a link between Ribera's
beggar subjects and the pictorial language of the
Bamboccianti. Besides parallels of motif, such as the ragged
garments of the figures, there is the patronage of the
viceroy the Duque de Alcalá, who evidently collected
works by both Pieter van Laer and Ribera and must have
seen something in common in them. However, the poetic
background landscapes and particularly the hazy sky
suggest Murillo rather than Ribera as an influence.

cities. Such discipline was exercised not just through police
enforcement and censorship but also by way of entirely
"modern" institutions such as effective courts and a
centrally co-ordinated welfare system for the poor, the first
step towards which had been taken in Naples with the
founding of the Pio Monte de la Misericordia. In this situation, the excessive use of force, noticeably waning elsewhere, as in contemporary Paris for example, continued to
scar everyday life in Naples. In the end, the dammed-up
forces of conflict burst forth with particularly gruesome
results in the Masaniello uprising of 1647/48. Although
the picture of the *Murder of Don Giuseppe Carafa* over-
dramatized matters in retrospect, it does show the ready
use of violence at the time (ill. 10). A subsequent major

turning point and new phase in the city's decline was the
plague epidemic of 1656, which reduced the population
of the kingdom of Naples to 1.8 million (ill. 11), a decrease
of 20 percent.

10 Domenico Gargiulo
The Murder of Don Giuseppe Carafa, 1656–1658
Oil on canvas, 29 x 38 cm
Museo Nazionale di San Martino, Naples

Domenico Gargiulo (1609–c. 1675), who was also known as Micco Spadaro, is the most important historical painter among Neapolitan artists. Several important events in the city's history were recorded by him in complicated figurative compositions. Like many of his local colleagues, he was trained in the studio of Aniello Falcone. There he became familiar with the etchings of Jacques Callot, which influenced him as much as the works of many other foreign artists whom he was able to study in the lively cultural atmosphere of contemporary Naples.

11 Domenico Gargiulo
The Piazza Mercatello during the Plague of 1656,
1656–1658
Oil on canvas, 126 x 177 cm
Museo Nazionale di San Martino, Naples

This picture was created along with two other historical paintings, one of which is devoted to the Masaniello uprising (ill. 59). Dietrich Erben presumes that the outbreak of plague prompted artists and clients alike to ponder the events of the previous ten years. The mounted figure in the foreground is possibly the viceroy in office at the time of the plague, who was later sharply criticized for his mistaken policies.

From Caravaggio's Chiaroscuro to a Naturalism Full of Color and Light

12 *St. Matthew with the Angel*, c. 1613
Oil on canvas, 86 x 69 cm
Great Art Inc., Tortola, Virgin Islands

This painting is to some extent a summation of the early Ribera. It has both the typical half-length figure of his Roman period, where the subject is separated from the viewer by a table. It also contains perhaps the clearest reference to Caravaggio in his entire oeuvre, borrowing the composition from the latter's painting of the same subject intended for the Contarelli chapel in San Luigi dei Francesi, which was rejected by the client. A feature of the picture by Ribera is also the lamentable state of the saint's reading matter, because in contrast to the Italian artist, Ribera prefers time and again to show well-used, sometimes even dog-eared books.

Ribera won the regard of leading contemporaries and art writers very quickly. In 1618 a Tuscan agent in Florence was already drawing attention to three astonishing pictures of saints by Ribera commissioned by the viceroy. The Bolognese painter Ludovico Carracci (1555–1619), who, together with his cousins Annibale (1560–1609) and Agostino (1557–1602), set the Baroque style on its way, enthused in extravagant terms in a letter written in December the same year about a now lost *St. Martin*, which Ribera had painted for the Farnese family in Parma.

The first biographical account of Ribera was written by the Roman physician Giulio Mancini († 1630) as early as 1620. A far more comprehensive life was written by Palomino de Castro y Velasco (1655–1726) as part of a collection of lives of Spanish artists. Published in 1724, Velasco's book formally followed the pattern of the famous collection of the lives of Italian artists by Giorgio Vasari (1511–1574). It was soon translated into other languages and therefore was significant in getting Spanish art known, even if Ribera's biography contains a number of slips. Given this relatively good supply of sources, it is surprising how little we know about the artist's early years. When the major expert on Spanish art, August L. Mayer, published a first critical catalog of Ribera's oeuvre, Palomino's assertion that the painter came from Játiva could not be proven. It was not until 1924 that the relevant documents were found, showing that the artist's father had been a cobbler in the town. It was, incidentally, an occupation very common among the Moriscos, i.e. the forcibly converted Muslims, in the area, who had little social prestige.

Játiva is not far from Valencia. Around 1600 it had a population of between 8,000 and 12,000, though even then it had a long history behind it. In Iberian times the town had been known as Saiti, which the Romans latinized as Saetabis. In 1563 the Dutch artist Anton van den Wyngaerde (c. 1525–1571) drew a vista of the town for Philip II (ill. 13).

Scholars are generally in agreement that the artist did not remain in Játiva but moved early in his career to Valencia, which was considered as a first-class cultural center at the time under Archbishop Juan de Ribera. In addition to the unambiguous references in numerous signatures mentioned earlier, there is a document dated 1622 concerning testimony by Ribera's brother Juan, who describes himself as a former resident of Valencia. It is conceivable that the brothers shared a house in the city, as it has been proven they did for the later period in Rome.

Accepting Palomino's biography, Mayer had assumed that Francisco Ribalta (1565–1628) was Ribera's teacher in Valencia. Ribalta played a key role in the development of the "Spanish school" in that in the course of his career he incorporated both traditional and progressive styles. Before settling in Valencia in 1599, he had lived in Madrid for 20 years and been in close contact there with the Italian artists, mostly from Florence and Rome, who had been imported to Spain by Philip. Besides their influence, other progressive styles and techniques can be traced in Ribalta's work, such as in his version of an earlier representation of the *Martyrdom of St. James* by Juan Fernández de Navarrete (c. 1526–1579), who was considered the most gifted Spanish artist at the Escorial and had learned much from Titian (c. 1485–1576) during a spell in Venice. With his gesture-laden figurative groups, Ribalta is still clearly in the Mannerist mode, yet he achieves individual characterizations of amazing quality, which were increasingly based on the observation of nature. Like the great innovative Baroque painter Caravaggio (1571–1610), who came from the Milan region (Lombardy), Ribalta used light to dramatize his pictorial subject. Whereas the Lombard was aiming at a naturalistic effect, however, Ribalta's purpose seems to have been to enhance the mystic, transcendental atmosphere.

We may thus confidently say that the techniques of observing nature and employment of light effects attracted renewed interest in Italy and Spain at almost the same time. Yet there were regional differences in the manner of implementation. These important observations are also relevant to the artistic classification of Ribera, because so far all attempts have failed to establish stylistic links (over and above vague similarities) between Ribera and Ribalta, in retrospect the two most important masters from Valencia. Not even any documentary evidence has been found in support of a link. In fact, the Játiva master could as easily have gleaned other important characteristics of his early

work, including the great lifelikeness of his figures and the intensity and expressiveness of their appearance, entirely from other Valencian artists of the time such as Juan Sariñena (c. 1545–1619) or Vicente Requena (c. 1556–c. 1607). There is therefore no compelling reason to follow scholars' usual practice and identify a single master as inspiration for Ribera. All that needs to be established is that while in Spain he was already being steered in a particular direction.

What then drove Ribera from Valencia and why did he go to Italy? The latter question is easier to answer than the former, because the Roman high renaissance was something of a legend along the Spanish Mediterranean coast and must have exercised a great fascination on a young artist. The Spanish scholar Miguel Morán presumes that the decision to leave Valencia could have been forced by political circumstances. Ribera could have turned his back on Valencia along with several other artists because an economic crisis had blown up following the final expulsion of the Moriscos in 1609/10.

If we turn to the question of his route to Italy, important for establishing artistic influences, the few known facts allow for two possible itineraries. The first mention of Ribera in Italy is the payment for *St. Martin* in Parma in 1611. The artist is then documented in Rome in 1613. Thus Ribera must either have gone by ship direct to Naples and from there to Parma and Rome, or taken the sea route from Barcelona to Genoa and then traveled overland through Lombardy towards the south. The second route was generally preferred at the time because of the threat from Muslim pirates.

Important in helping to reconstruct the early creative years of Ribera are the stylistic features of his pictures and the relevant assessments in contemporary sources. As the Parma *St. Martin* is only known to us through a

copy and an etching, the ranks of pictures for consideration must begin with the works that were probably done in Rome. In this respect, the best-known group are the *Allegories of the Five Senses*, which some recent research puts as early as 1613. This establishes a time framework for the other works. Of the other Ribera paintings dated to this period, two subjects merit particular attention because they relate directly to previous treatments by Caravaggio, namely Ribera's various versions of *St. Jerome* (ill. 15) and his *St. Matthew with the Angel* (ill. 12). The comparative pictures by Caravaggio are likewise a *St. Matthew with the Angel,* specifically the first and second versions of the picture he painted for the Contarelli chapel of San Luigi dei Francesi in Rome (the first version was destroyed in the Second World War), and his two versions of *St. Jerome* now in Rome (ill. 16) and Malta. In Caravaggio's first version of *St. Matthew with the Angel,* the immediate striking feature is the unusual relationship between the saint and the angel, which indeed caused the artist's client to reject the picture. Not only does the saint look extremely clumsy in the way he writes, the angel also looks rather disrespectful.

He appears to be crowding the evangelist in an attempt to guide his hand. Ribera's version of the subject (ill. 12) is markedly more conventional, but there is an astonishing similarity in the heads of the two saints, and also the angel is once again very close to the main figure, giving the impression that he too wants to read the book.

The pictorial subject of St. Jerome was not an innovation of either Caravaggio or Ribera, and neither artist was able to add basically new features to his iconography. Nonetheless, St. Jerome, along with St. Bartholomew, became a kind of trade mark for the Spanish artist. There are two different arrangements for the presentation of St. Jerome: one was as the scholar at

13 Anton van den Wyngaerde
Prospect of Játiva, 1563
Pen, brown ink and water color on paper, 28.2 x 104.7 cm
Öesterreichische Nationalbibliothek, Cod. Min. 41, fol. 70, Vienna

Several documents and Ribera's own references on his pictures prove that he came from the Spanish town of Játiva. The town was the oldest center of paper production, but owed its economic prosperity mainly to extensive fruit growing. The Moors, who occupied the town from 711, had developed an ingenious system of terraces and irrigation channels, which remained in place after the Christian re-conquest in 1239. The gardens continued to be run by Moriscos, who in Ribera's early years constituted about a sixth of the town's population.

14 Annibale Carracci
Man Eating Beans, c. 1584
Oil on canvas, 78 x 95 cm
Galleria Colonna, Rome

This picture by Annibale Carracci displays astonishing parallels to Ribera's *Allegories of the Senses* in both composition and iconography. In both cases, we find an ordinary person taken from everyday life as a half-length figure, behind a table on which various objects are placed as in a still life. A particular interest in such genre subjects, which were especially favored in the Netherlands, was manifest most strongly in Lombardy in northern Italy, which was the home of both Annibale Carracci and Caravaggio.

work in his study, a type that prevailed in the 16th century as the perfect embodiment of the humanist ideal and was definitively depicted by Albrecht Dürer (1471–1528) in one of his "master engravings". The other type shows the visionary ascetic in the desert, with his numerous attributes from earlier representations being reduced to the core features of a crucifix, a skull and a lion.

In his version now in the Galleria Borghese, Caravaggio combined both types while also incorporating features from a further tradition, namely that of the philosopher (ill. 16). The result is a saint poring over his books, wholly absorbed in his studies. Thanks to the subtle lighting, his bald pate is optically equivalent to the skull representing mortality.

In contrast, Ribera's preference is for the visionary ascetic type (ill. 15), but in some versions of the subject he places an angel from the Last Judgment alongside the main figure where once again we may assume that the source was Caravaggio, namely the second version of *St. Matthew with the Angel*, which is now in San Luigi dei Francesi.

Ribera also makes use of Caravaggio's version of *St. Jerome* in which the scholar is shown in an impoverished environment alone with his books as the beggar philosopher. We can fairly conclude that the artistic influence of the celebrated Lombard painter is a distinctive element in the early work of Ribera that reappears to a certain extent in his later work.

Contemporary sources likewise frequently connect Caravaggio's name with Ribera. In the letter of 1618 mentioned earlier, Ludovico Carracci mentions a Spanish painter who was influenced by the school of Caravaggio: "pittore, Spagnuolo, che tiene dietro alla scuola di Caravaggio," and Palomino writes in his life: "He orientated himself strongly on the school of Caravaggio, and mastered his splendid chiaroscuro style, making progress every day with the constantly repeated imitation of nature."

So when did Ribera first come into contact with the work of the Lombard master? Although several works now in Spain are attributed to Caravaggio or are, clearly inspired by him, initially at least there appear to have been few actual examples to see, although admittedly there was an accessible copy of the *Crucifixion of St. Peter* in Valencia in the possession of the archbishop and art patron Juan de Ribera. The situation was very different in Italy, where the Spanish artist certainly saw the first version of the picture of *St. Matthew with the Angel*, then still in the collection of Prince Vincenzo Giustiniani. This picture acted as a direct inspiration for him.

Even today, as has already been briefly indicated in the case of Ribera and Ribalta, art historians are inclined to apply hindsight to link great names in supposed teacher–pupil relationships. In reality, the situation was much more complicated. Important artists are not necessarily good teachers, nor good

16 Caravaggio
St. Jerome, c. 1606
Oil on canvas, 112 x 157 cm
Museo Galleria Borghese, Rome

In contemporary sources, the name of Caravaggio is
mentioned again and again in connection with Ribera.
However, the subject of St. Jerome was already popular
with 16th-century artists long before Caravaggio's time.

15 (facing page)
St. Jerome and the Angel of the Last Judgment, 1626
Oil on canvas, 262 x 164 cm
Museo di Capodimonte, Naples

In the 17th century, Ribera's art was already becoming
closely associated with his depictions of St. Jerome.
Various versions of the saint (here seen reacting with a
gesture of pathos to the apocalyptic clarion of the Last
Trumpet) are found in Osuna (Seville), St. Petersburg and
Naples. As a rule, contemporaries were not familiar with
these pictures in the originals but via an etching made in
1621, the most successful of Ribera's printed graphics.

teachers important artists. The same applies in this
case: it was not so much Caravaggio himself who was
the key factor for Ribera as the new style of art that he
initiated. Caravaggio was a loner who jealously discour-
aged imitators. Presumably his style fell on fertile
ground with the Spanish artist because Ribera had
already become acquainted with the new visual armory
of enhanced naturalism and dramatic chiaroscuro in
Spain and during his journey to Rome.

Ribera definitely spent some time in Parma. Not
very far away, but already part of the Church state, the
city of Bologna was the home of Annibale Carracci,
the most important of the founders of Baroque
painting mentioned earlier. Carracci's 1584 painting of
the *Man Eating Beans* (ill. 14) has left us early testimony to his vivid observation of everyday life. If
Ribera did indeed take the northern route on his
journey through Italy, he probably passed through
Milan, which at that time was also under Spanish rule.
Milan was the home of a special approach to reality

painting. Caravaggio was by no means the inventor of
the new "naturalistic" style, but he was the carrier that
took the typical visual language of his Lombardy
homeland to the south of Italy.

Finally, Ribera's Roman connections must have been
of paramount importance to him. As in international
art centers in other countries and times, the most
fruitful contacts were not between foreign and Italian
artists but initially among the foreigners themselves.
Caravaggio's new style met with a particularly warm
welcome among the new arrivals, as is clear from the
relevant works by Dirk Baburen (c. 1594/95–1624,
arr. in Rome 1612/13), Gerrit van Honthorst
(c. 1590/92–1656, in Rome 1610–1612), the Frenchman Valentin de Boulogne (1594–1632) and Simon
Vouet (1590–1649, both arriving in Rome 1613/14).
Like Ribera, all these artists relied on the same patrons,
for example the Genoese banker Giustiniani.

We know that in 1615 Ribera was living with Spaniards and Flemings in the Via Margutta in Rome. This

was a natural community in that they were all part of the Hispanic world. Caravaggio's *tenebrismo* had already become a subject of much debate among them in 1613, and there are good grounds for thinking Ribera, who had already adopted the style, was involved from the first. The contacts with artists in Valencia, his stay in northern Italy, and finally the association with northern Italian Caravaggists in Rome undoubtedly excited the naturalistic interest of the young Spanish artist much more than a single painting by Caravaggio could have done. Even then, other sources seem to have inspired him. Other influences are clearly evident in his treatment of landscapes (especially in the early work) and first became obvious in his picture of *Jacob and Laban's Flock* (ill. 18) of 1632.

The composition of the picture and the portrait of Jacob do indeed follow Caravaggian principles, but the subtle use of light that imbues all solid matter and evokes conspicuous reflections on the wool of the sheep indicates an interest in the neo-Venetian fashion in Rome. In fact, it could well suggest an acquaintance with the work of the influential Genoese artist Giovanni Benedetto Castiglione (1609–1664), who was active in Rome at this time. Nonetheless, even in Ribera's late oeuvre there are still works where the artist drew again on this "tenebrism" because it seemed better suited to certain subjects such as the nocturnal *Adoration of the Shepherds*. In this, Ribera showed his independence of stylistic fashions. Although he naturally paid due respect to changing tastes among his patrons, he steered clear of slavish adherence to fashion. The naturalistic vein runs through his entire

oeuvre like a red thread, from the *Allegories of the Five Senses* (c. 1613) via the "beggar philosophers" (c. 1630) to the two late versions of the *Adoration of the Shepherds* (1640).

Nonetheless, it should be noted at this point that, whereas Caravaggio was the flag-bearer for chiaroscuro, Ribera became, in Mayer's words, the "prophet of light". A new quality of light can be discerned early on in his work, with an amber-colored sheen on the body of his figures, as well as in many aspects of his treatment of landscapes, and after 1632 we find the typical silver-grey coloration of his mature style in many of his pictures.

Though Ribera's connection with Caravaggio and especially with the latter's followers, the Caravaggists, is accepted by all scholars, opinions differ about the artistic sources of the second phase of his oeuvre after 1632. Italian writers in particular detect on the one hand the influences of the Flemish painter Antony van Dyck (1599–1641), who traveled through Italy from 1621–1627, and spent some time in Palermo; and on the other the Venetian painters Titian (c. 1485–1576) and Veronese (Paolo Caliari, 1528–1588), who had been rediscovered by Castiglione and his associates in contemporary Rome. Other art historians prefer to account for the change of style in Ribera's work with the influence of the classical painters, above all Guido Reni (1575–1642). The latter critics can at least cite the fact that Reni's influence is to some degree already discernible in the early work of our painter and is mentioned in contemporary sources as a model for Ribera quite as frequently as Caravaggio.

17 *Jacob and Laban's flock* (detail of ill. 18)

Meticulous observation and representation of details were a speciality of Dutch art. The northern Italians and Spaniards who had followed its example reduced the motifs but displayed no lesser talent for naturalistic representation. In this case it is the still, smooth surface of the pond which captures in its lifelikeness: the head of the sheep is reflected for a moment before it begins to drink.

18 *Jacob and Laban's flock*, 1632
Oil on canvas, 174 x 219 cm
Patrimonio Nacional, Monasterio de San Lorenzo de El
Escorial

The date of 1632, which re-emerged with the most recent
cleaning of the painting, confirms the key role of this work
within Ribera's artistic development. In it we encounter a
new concept of lighting for the first time, probably
inspired by neo-Venetian influences in Rome.
The accomplished integration of Jacob and his animals
into the landscape, plus the diagonal axis of movement,
give the picture an unusual dynamism not found in
earlier works.

Revisiting the Beginnings of the Allegories of the Five Senses

19 Anonymous
Allegory of Hearing (copy after Ribera)
Oil on canvas, 114 x 79 cm
Europahaus, Vienna

With the *Allegories of the Five Senses*, Ribera created the most successful pictorial series of his early works. Four of the originals have been located. Only Ribera's original of the *Allegory of Hearing* is missing.

20 (facing page)
Allegory of Sight, c. 1613
Oil on canvas, 114 x 89 cm
Museo Franz Mayer, Mexico City

In his representations of the five senses, Ribera followed contemporary humanistic rankings. The higher value put on sight is made clear in the allegory by the characterization of the figure and the rather valuable objects. Yet the half-length figure conveys a rather contradictory message. In contrast to the intelligent facial features, the hands are not in the least dainty and have black fingernails, like those of a manual worker. The clothing is fine enough but scarcely indicative of wealth.

One of the most informative texts about the early Ribera comes from Giulio Mancini, physician to Pope Urban VIII. In his *Considerazioni sulla Pittura* (1614–1621), which was widely disseminated in manuscript form and very influential, he records not only important biographical information but also names individual works and gives his own assessments. In his view, Ribera had to leave Parma because many people envied him his position at the Farnese court. He likewise sees the move from Rome to Naples as an enforced decision brought about by an expensive lifestyle and its consequent mountain of debt. In Mancini's eyes, Ribera was not only one of the most gifted artists for many years but also a real bohemian who more than once had difficulties with his creditors: "Here in Rome he was rather liberal in his behavior and although very clever, he still sometimes got into difficulties. ... And indeed, we may say he found it easy to act in bad faith, because when he wished to work, he earned five or six scudi a day, so that if his expenses had been normal, he could have paid everyone easily and quickly. But with all the extravagance he soon spent at least this amount. ... Nonetheless, he had a very good reputation. And what was astonishing, he could turn on the friendly words with men who had a taste for pictures and were moneylenders, using a fluent tongue, words and tricks to give them hope of [his] doing what they wanted. The big landowners, bakers, butchers, greengrocers and Jews on the other hand banged at his door and sent bailiffs with *citationi* in the middle of the night, so that in the end he left Rome for fear of the possible consequences."

As these lines by Mancini show, despite his early success Ribera had constant money difficulties that caused him and his family considerable problems in later years when he was also professionally hampered by illness. Ironically, this paradoxical situation is rather like a mirror image of the Spanish state, which from the time of Philip II's accession was permanently on the edge of bankruptcy despite the constant flow of new wealth brought by the silver ships from Latin America. In a biographical connection, these latent situations of crisis for the highly successful Ribera can, however, be interpreted as confirmation of an uncommon social rise that clearly caused the cobbler's

son more problems than they did for a painter like Caravaggio, for example, who came from a so-called "good" family.

It is also instructive to see which of Ribera's works Mancini expressly singles out at the end of his text: "He did many things in Rome and especially for ... [there follows an illegible name] the Spaniard, who possesses five wonderful half-length figures representing the five senses, a Deposition and others that are indeed things of exquisite beauty [*cose di esquisitissima bellezza*]." Whereas the "Deposition" has been identified by the scholar José Milicua as that in the Louvre, it was not until the 1960s that the *Allegories of the Five Senses* were identified with the relevant pictures by Roberto Longhi (ills. 2, 20, 21, 23). At the time, Longhi argued largely on the basis of copies (ill. 19), but since then four of the five originals have been found. The great number of later versions may be a clear indication of the extraordinary success of the series. Several of the copies are currently in Spanish collections, further proof of the early influence of the Spanish artist's new pictorial language in his homeland.

Mancini begins his text with astonishing praise for Ribera: "We can and should not deny that Giuseppe Ribera from Valencia, who is generally called Lo Spagnoletto, is the most naturally talented artist [*una disposition tale da natura*] to have appeared here for years." With these words, Mancini clearly sets him above all the other artists then pouring into Rome and adopting the new pictorial language of Caravaggio, because at this time Mancini can only have known works in which Ribera likewise came to grips with the Lombard artist's "tenebrism." In the subsequent course of his brief biography, the artistically minded physician even goes a step further in confirming that the artist largely followed Caravaggio's example in the use of color but "was bolder and more ready to experiment." It is therefore worth investigating the example of the *Allegories of the Five Senses* to establish just what does distinguish early Ribera from Caravaggio.

All the works in this first known phase of Ribera's career, for example the *St. Matthew with the Angel* already mentioned (ill. 12), display not only technical correspondences with Caravaggio but also an amazing homogeneity of composition, in each case linking the

22 Caravaggio
Madonna of Loreto, 1605
Oil on canvas, 260 x 150 cm
Sant' Agostino, Rome

The artist confines his representation to the essentials. Instead of showing how the angels carry the Virgin's house to Loreto – the miracle at the heart of the pilgrimages to Loreto – he only shows us the contrast between the Christian beauty of the Madonna and the dirt of the travelling pilgrims, who have come a long way and are clearly poor. In this reduction, and in the generic nature of the scene, there is a parallel with Ribera's compositional concept for the *Allegories of the Five Senses*. But whereas Caravaggio threatens to overstep the limits of *decoro* – the Christ child appears all too human and we can clearly see the Virgin's bare feet – the Spanish artist ran no such risks with his secular themes.

21 (facing page)
Allegory of Smell, c. 1613
Oil on canvas, 115 x 88 cm
Abello Collection, Madrid

The artist selects an altogether contrary symbolism to the traditional allegory of smell. Instead of desirable scents, generally symbolized with bottles of fine perfume and exquisite flowers, Ribera evokes the smells of garlic and onions that bring tears to the beggar's eyes. Restricting the depiction to just a few objects has parallels in the Spanish genre of *bodegón* painting.

23 *Allegory of Taste*, c. 1613
Oil on canvas, 113.5 x 87.5 cm
Wadsworth Atheneum, Hartford

The coarse facial expression of Ribera's noodle-eater, whose shirt barely meets across his chest and belly, and who clutches his valuable glass somewhat clumsily by the base in his fist, has no parallel in Caravaggio's art. Though the Lombard painter also sought models among the poor, not even the *Supper at Emmaus*, which deals most closely with a comparable genre subject among the religious works, shows similar closeness to the subject.

two genres of still life and lifelike portraiture. Highly expressive half-length figures sit behind tables on which various everyday objects are always arranged like precious artifacts. In the case of the *Allegories of the Five Senses*, conformity with the social hierarchy is observable in the characterization of the figures, which clearly goes hand in hand with the contemporary ranking of the senses. Whereas the figure that personifies the more noble visual sense (ill. 20) is endowed with (among other things) a telescope and pince-nez, the figure for the lower-ranking sense of taste has a plate in front of him (ill. 23) that at first sight looks full of worms. They are in fact noodles. In addition, the subject is wearing earrings, an unmistakable indication to contemporaries that he is a gypsy.

With the *Allegories of the Five Senses*, Ribera adopted a theme that already looked back on an established tradition and some outstanding paintings, for example the famous series by Jan Brueghel the Elder (1568–1625) now in the Prado. The special quality of Ribera's series lies in the painter's ability to give a new slant to an old pictorial subject by the choice of models and introduction of an unusual symbolism. The depiction of the blind man in the *Allegory of Touch* (ill. 2) and the use of an onion instead of the hitherto customary flower as a symbol of smell (ill. 21) are examples of Ribera's innovative approach to his theme.

The extreme naturalism and chiaroscuro painting show clearly the influence of Caravaggio. Comparing Ribera's allegory of taste (ill. 23) with the first version of Caravaggio's *Supper at Emmaus* of 1596 makes for an interesting contrast. In both cases we find the main figure placed between a table with objects arranged as in a still life and a brownish-grey wall, which is illuminated by light coming from top left. Both the body of Christ and the allegorical figure gain immeasurable depth by the use of "tenebrism", and even the movements of the hand correspond. However, the differences are also significant. In Caravaggio, food is only an accessory in a composition determined entirely by dramatic gestures, whereas in Ribera a meal is given a fundamental role. With the former, we find dishes arranged artfully as on a buffet, in Ribera everything is being used. Yet the greatest difference is in the dour phenotypes of Ribera's protagonists.

Indeed, in Caravaggio's work there is no comparable example where everyday protagonists are allowed as much room for self-representation or where due respect is paid to them in comparable fashion. Though Caravaggio sometimes does use models from the lower social classes, he generally robs them of their identity by dressing them in unusual costumes or linking them into existing hierarchies, as with the two pilgrims kneeling before the *Madonna of Loreto* (ill. 22).

In contrast, Ribera shows respect not only for his figures but also for the objects assigned to them. He presents these not as lifeless objects, but makes their use part of the subject matter. For example, if we compare his depictions of books with those of Caravaggio, it is striking that in Ribera there is no text that does not look read a hundred times and thoroughly

absorbed from repeated use. The Lombard gives his pictures a setting, whereas the Spaniard shares his observations with us and tests them time and again against real life.

The parallels between Ribera's view of people and things and the investigations of Galileo have quite rightly been noted by historians. Both seek a direct access to reality that was new for the time, thereby relying more on their own eyes than on the doctrine of tradition. Possibly there are more connections over and above this than have hitherto been assumed. The inventor of the *cannochiale* (telescope) that Ribera was the first to put in a painting (ill. 20), Galileo was in Rome in 1611 and again in 1615/16. It is conceivable that Ribera learned of his pioneering investigations in the city where they took place. The pince-nez in the *Allegory of Sight* (ills. 20, 26) on the other hand indicates the great role that glasses began to play in the Hispanic world from the 16th century. The social elite flashed them about as status symbols, presumably with the intention of breaking down the confines within which personal images had to operate under the strict Spanish dress code.

As regulations provided for black fabrics only and banned all forms of the lace so popular elsewhere at the time, anyone who wanted to be noticed had to resort to unusual means. No-one caught the extravagances of spectacle fever on canvas so neatly as Ribera in his portrait of a *Knight of the Order of St. James* (ill. 25). The white highlights on the impressive sash, an indication of the subject's membership of the Spanish party in the Thirty Years' War, already indicate the artist's second period, enabling us to date the picture to the mid-1630s.

Once we have established the particular naturalism in Ribera's art compared with Caravaggio – the interest in earthy typicality and at the same time respect for others and their world, plus an emphasis on the utility value of objects and a fascination for light – it becomes clear how closely Ribera stands to Velázquez's work. If, following the latest research, we date the *Allegories of the Five Senses* to 1613, it is possible they served as models for works included among the *bodegones* such as *The Water Seller of Seville* (ill. 24) of 1622.

Characteristically, in his posthumous treatise on art, *Arte de la Pintura*, Velázquez's father-in-law Francisco Pacheco (1564–1644) mentions the three painters Michelangelo Merisi da Caravaggio, Diego Velázquez and Jusepe de Ribera in one breath when it comes to the challenge of the closest possible study of nature:

"But I stick to nature in everything; and the best thing would be if I could always have her in front of me at all times, not just for heads, nudes, hands and feet but also for clothes and silks and everything else. That's how Michelangelo Caravaggio did it; you can see how successful it is in the Crucifixion of St. Peter (although these are copies); that is how Jusepe de Ribera does it, since among all the important paintings that the Duque de Alcalá possesses his figures and heads appear to be alive, the others just painted, even alongside Guido of Bologna; and in the work of my

24 Diego Velázquez
The Water Seller of Seville, c. 1622
Oil on canvas, 106.7 x 81 cm
Wellington Museum, Apsley House, London

There are many reasons for considering the *Allegories of the Five Senses* an important source for Velázquez's *bodegones*. The latter are a peculiarly Spanish form of still life in which figures could also appear. They were among Velázquez's favorite subjects during his early period in Seville. With this picture and its brilliant effects, Velázquez put his virtuosity on view, thereby gaining the desired attention of the Spanish court. The heroic representation of a simple man – there were water sellers in Spain until quite recently – has been interpreted as an ideological reference to the persecution of people of other creeds by the Inquisition. However the pictures themselves reveal more of Velázquez's and Ribera's closeness to everyday culture, inherent in their origins and their respect for a social class they grew from and left behind as a result of their artistic success.

26 *Allegory of Sight* (detail of ill. 20)

Ribera took particular care to cultivate his contacts with artists from northern countries, and one is tempted to recognize their strict analytical eye in the selection and representation of the symbolic objects in the *Allegories of the Five Senses*. The presentation has little in common with Caravaggio's still lifes. The meager selection is certainly a Spanish feature, because we find a similar deliberate restriction in the *bodegón* genre. In this picture we are shown a mirror, a pince-nez and what is presumably the case belonging to it. The pince-nez, along with the telescope (a further aid to sight), may also be intended as an allusion to the amazing predilection among Spaniards for conspicuous glasses, which were used as status symbols, especially among the upper crust.

25 (facing page)
Knight of the Order of St. James, 1637–1640
Oil on canvas, 146 x 107 cm
Algur H Meadows Collection, Meadows Museum,
Southern Methodist University, Dallas

This subject has not yet been conclusively identified, but he is furnished with a multitude of attributes that inform us not only of his membership of the respected Order of St. James the Great (he has the red cross of the Order on the shells of St. James on the chain) but also his high military rank. Besides the glasses there is also the stiff ruff, which had been in fashion at the Spanish court since 1623 and remained so until Ribera's death, and which shows him as a man of fashion.

son-in-law, who does it the same way, you can see the difference from the others, because he always has nature before him."

All three artists – Caravaggio, Ribera and Velázquez – did intensive studies on human models for their early work, and show us the results not in an architectural space but in front of a neutral background structured only by means of chiaroscuro. But over and above these formal parallels, there are also similarities of subject matter. Time and again we encounter half-length figures from secular contexts at their work. They not only appear very close to the viewer but with their gaze seem to address us quite specifically. Often only a table lends distance between them and us.

In this respect it is perhaps Caravaggio who goes furthest with his pictures of boys, whose homoerotic radiance clearly breaks taboos of the time. In comparison, the works of Velázquez seem thoroughly reserved. Though his figures are simple folk, they exude an uncommon degree of repose and distinction that scarcely tallies with the rest of their image. It can easily be imagined that in this respect Ribera was the link between the extremes of the other two artists.

WORKS FOR THE DUKE OF OSUNA – WHY RENI IS AN INADEQUATE EXPLANATION

27 *Calvary*, 1616–1618
Oil on canvas, 336 x 230 cm
Patronato de Art, Osuna (Seville)

Even in this early work we find a typical feature of Ribera's art: both his mythological and his religious figures always possess an earthiness anchored in reality. Their definition over and above that is made clear by a handful of attributes. Instead of the eyes directed heavenwards as in Reni, in Ribera we find introverted or even veiled gazes; his protagonists appear to be working out their own destinies.

According to Mancini, Ribera's move to Naples also solved his monetary problems. With his usual luck, he was immediately introduced to the viceroy, the Duke of Osuna, who ruled from 1616 (the year of Ribera's arrival) to 1620. "The result was that he continued to live in the city with his usual expenses plus those required to maintain a wife and an honorable appearance at court. Even so, he had left the extravagances behind him, and his rapid working methods in painting and his discernment helped him to arrange his earnings adequately to maintain the splendor of his lifestyle."

There are differing reports as to how the Duke of Osuna and Ribera became acquainted and developed mutual esteem. The important Neapolitan art writer Bernardo de Dominici (1683–1759) records an anecdote in which the viceroy was looking from the balcony of his palace and saw a great crowd attracted to a public presentation of one of Ribera's pictures. The "attractiveness" of this *St. Bartholomew* (ill. 28) was attributed by the author "as much to the appropriate depiction of the tragic subject matter as to the novelty of the style." The most informative part of the text is at the end, where it is reported that the Duke "wanted to see the picture, and when it was brought to him, he liked it so much that he also had the painter summoned. As he usually did, Ribera had written his name on the picture and added *español*, perhaps just in order to carry out this trick. It worked, because the viceroy praised him greatly and wanted to have the picture himself, and only days later named him court painter..."

Even if this anecdote was apocryphal – Ribera was never court painter in the classic sense – it shows that the Neapolitan de Dominici already perceived Ribera's reference to his Spanish origin as self-advertisement. That artists used public exhibitions to get future patrons interested in them seems to have been a normal procedure. Velázquez too is supposed to have initially obtained his position as court painter and later the important commission for the portrait of Pope Innocent X in this way.

The picture mentioned by de Dominici was long considered lost, but is today identified with a work now in Osuna. There it forms a part of a group of five works by Ribera, all of which the widow of the viceroy donated to the local collegiate church in 1627. The family vault is in the same church. The other pictures show a *St. Sebastian* (ill. 29), a St. Jerome, a St. Peter in prayer and a *Calvary* (ill. 27). Four of them were inserted into a baroque high altar in 1770 and were crudely restored and trimmed during this process.

Although the *Calvary* was long dated later, it is now assumed that all the pictures were painted between 1616 and 1618, and thus form the first great group of works after the *Allegories of the Five Senses*. Consequently the *Allegories* are used again and again by scholars as a principal point of comparison for the pictures in Osuna. Various sources are incorporated in the three portraits of saints and two narrative scenes. The individuality of Ribera's style is now expressed in his combining Caravaggesque chiaroscuro with elements from the Roman and Bolognan classical style.

In the works for the Duke of Osuna, and particularly in the *Calvary* scene, these influences can be elucidated in exemplary fashion. Caravaggio's influence is evident in the lighting, with its strongly sculptural effect, the figural types and the rich detail. A typical example is the presentation of the arm muscles in the picture of *St. Bartholomew* (ill. 28), reminiscent of an anatomy demonstration. On the other hand, the influence of the Romano-Bolognan classical style can be felt in the strict composition and more intense coloration, and also in the use of classical models for the nude figure. The background landscapes with their sparse vegetation and horizontal strips of cloud in an intense blue sky, already familiar from the *Allegory of Sight* (ill. 20), go back to Roman and Bolognese models.

That the two artistic approaches of naturalism and the classical style were not irreconcilable Ribera could have observed for himself especially in the example of Guido Reni. Reni, who came from Bologna, was a leading figure in the development of the Baroque style. Even in the 17th century he was considered an innovator in the handling of color and light, and he exercised considerable influence on other artists in his environment. It therefore comes as no surprise that there are a number of references in contemporary sources to a connection between Ribera and Reni. Mancini himself reported that Ribera was considered

29 *St. Sebastian*, 1616–1618
Oil on canvas, 179 x 139 cm
Patronato de Arte, Osuna (Seville)

Many source texts for Ribera refer to a fairly close
relationship between the artist and Guido Reni, a leading
representative of Romano–Bolognese classicism. In
practice, the influence is possibly traceable in only a
handful of works. In the case of *St. Sebastian*, the figure
of the saint shows a sense of balance and harmony
reminiscent of classical models of antiquity, and the sharp
edges of the folds of drapery in the loin cloth could have
been borrowed from relevant models.

28 (facing page)
St. Bartholomew, 1616-1618
Oil on canvas, 179 x 139 cm
Patronato de Arte, Osuna (Seville)

This picture may have been crudely trimmed in order to
fit into a Baroque high altar. In the process, an inscription
and putti placing a crown on the martyr's head, mentioned
by the Neapolitan writer De Dominici, may have been
lost. It can, however, be definitely stated that the male
figure behind the executioner, who now looks out of the
picture, originally had a counterpart.

an admirer of Guido Reni, and particularly stressed his
"decisiveness and his handling of color." Another
important art biographer, Filippo Baldinucci (1625–
1697), wrote that in Rome Ribera particularly copied
works by Reni and learned freshness of coloration from
him; and finally Palomino also declared Ribera to be an
emulator of the Bolognese artist. We cannot wonder
therefore that art historian Alfonso E. Pérez Sánchez
even presumes that Ribera got to know Reni in

Bologna on his journey from Spain to Italy and later
met him in Rome and Naples.

Of the Osuna paintings, Reni's influence has been
cited principally in the *St. Sebastian* (ill. 29) and
Calvary (ill. 27). The comparison of Ribera's *Calvary*
with the picture on the same subject by Reni, probably
only completed a year later (ill. 31), seems overrated by
scholars. In contrasting them, we need to bear in mind
that the Spanish artist's picture has suffered greatly over

30 *Calvary* (detail of ill. 27)

Although the heads of the Virgin and St. John face
different directions and there is no eye contact between the
two figures, the junction of the diagonals in their markedly
different postures brings them together compositionally
as a group. Ribera shows each person beneath the Cross as
being alone with his sorrow; but together, so the painter
suggests, they will have the strength to spread the belief
in Christ.

the centuries. Napoleon's troops used the painting for
target practice and after its restoration a figure not
unimportant to the composition vanished in the darkness on the right.

It is true that in both Ribera and Reni we find a still
living Christ who directs his gaze towards Heaven,
seeking help, but the people beneath the Cross are
treated fundamentally differently. In Ribera's composition the three remaining figures embody on the one
hand highly individual displays of grief and yet on the
other their postures form a physically closed group. The
coloration of their garments is highly variegated and
intense, reminiscent of Venetian models. Since Titian's
day at least, coloration had enjoyed a greater esteem in
Venice than in Rome, where drawing was more highly
valued. In particular, the blue in Mary's mantle and the
green in Mary Magdelene's are unusual for the time, but
are repeated in other pictures by Ribera. In Reni,
composition and the use of color are quite different: the
figures of the Virgin Mary and St. John are symmetri-
cally positioned and both gaze heavenwards, while the
robes of all three figures are uniform in coloration and
look little differentiated in the drapery.

Certainly Reni will have given Ribera much food for
thought, but he was not his central point of reference.
Pacheco himself defends Ribera against this false
assumption with his words "even alongside Guido of
Bologna" in the passage quoted above. Reni's predominant influence was an assumption rarely made by
contemporaries, but it found great favor among Italian
art writers of the late 17th and 18th centuries with
their strong attachment to classical painting.

Pacheco was in an excellent position to appreciate
Ribera's art in fine detail, as his son-in-law Velázquez
was probably able to speak to Ribera in 1630. The fall
of the Duke of Osuna in 1620 prevented his giving any
further commissions, but Ribera had become so
famous in the meantime that he now found plenty of
other customers for his work. It thus caused him no
hardship that the next two viceroys generally displayed
little interest in art and therefore failed to ply him with
commissions or financial contributions. Instead of the
artificial taste of a restricted court elite, throughout the
1620s Ribera's work reflects more general stylistic
trends that appeared in the religious and mythological
painting of the time, and not only in Naples.

31 Guido Reni (facing page)
Crucifixion of the Capuchin, 1619
Oil on canvas, 397 x 266 cm
Pinacoteca Nazionale, Bologna

If we accept the new dating for Ribera's pictures in Osuna,
the possibility that Reni's *Crucifixion* served as a model for
him is excluded on chronological grounds. In fact, the
pictures have far less in common than the frequent
comparisons suggest. This applies both to the arrangement
of the figures beneath the Cross and the choice of colors.
Unlike Ribera, Reni uses large areas and homogeneous
forms to shape the clothing. Highlights are provided
instead by the strongly differentiated flesh tones of each
person. His *Crucifixion of the Capuchin* awoke great
interest in Rome, but nevertheless its claimed effect on
Ribera has yet to be demonstrated.

Confessionalization and Religious Propaganda Pictures

32 *Martyrdom of St. Bartholomew*, 1644 [?]
Oil on canvas, 202 x 153 cm
Museu Nacional d'Art de Catalunya, Barcelona

It is noticeable in the works of Ribera that there is always at least one figure in direct eye contact with the viewer. The example of St. Bartholomew is particularly insistent in this respect. Shown by the artist in almost horizontal position, he has his mouth and his eyes wide open, fixed upon the viewer, while the executioner sets about his business of torture with a sadistic smirk.

It is customary to classify Baroque religious painting as the direct expression of the ideas formulated at the Council of Trent (1545–1563), when the leading powers in the Catholic world, namely the Pope, the French and Spanish kings and the German emperor, agreed the principles of joint religious policy for the future. The much-invoked decree concerning the legitimacy of images, resolved only during the final session of the Council at the insistence of France, which found itself particularly under threat from the iconoclastic Calvinists, only provided a very general framework. Only breaches of *decoro* – perhaps best translated as religious seemliness – by indecency or lascivious depictions in church interiors, were expressly denounced. For the rest, the competent bishops of the time had the final say as to whether a work of art could be shown publicly or not. More important than the Tridentine guidelines, therefore, were the regional regulations for their implementation, and these continued to take very different forms.

The movement hitherto generally known as the Counter-Reformation, which only apparently coincided with the Council of Trent, was not just a response to the Reformation. It constituted in effect only one of several religious reform movements in the 16th century that ultimately sprang from similar premises. A more appropriate term than the concepts of counter-reformation or Catholic reform is a word relatively new to historiography, namely "confessionalism," as proposed by the historian Heinz Schilling. Clerical leaders such as Jean Calvin (1509–1564), Martin Luther (1483–1546) and the founder of the Jesuit order Ignatius Loyola (1491–1556) had common objectives. They wanted to propagate their own religious ideas by using strict social control mechanisms, thus achieving a uniformity of creed among their respective followers.

In the kingdom of Naples, religious traditions of the Papacy and Spain mingled. Contrary to the view put forward by Protestant historians, both had begun to reform their concepts of faith even before the appearance of Luther, but the picture that emerges is to some extent one of very diverse attitudes, as is indicated by the debate about the immaculate conception of the Virgin – an important subject also for Ribera. Naples thus became a kind of "laboratory of Catholic confes-sionalization," i.e. a place where suitable artistic means to standardize concepts of faith were tried out.

Ribera's saints are, as a rule, neither recent candidates for sainthood nor the recently canonized but rather well-enough known figures who are shown in a novel way, like St. Bartholomew, who was reputedly flayed alive for his Christian faith. Key iconographical elements in the presentation of St. Bartholomew already feature in the picture done for the Duke of Osuna (ill. 28). They include the figure of the saint tied to a tree stump wearing only a loincloth for covering, in a dramatic setting heightened by the lighting and the presence of an executioner, whose brutality and heartlessness are evident from the all too obvious flaying knife. Also among Ribera's standard repertoire are a number of non-participant standing figures facing each other in the background. In the picture of *The Martyrdom of St. Bartholomew* (ill. 35) now in the Palazzo Pitti in Florence, two further elements also feature: first, the suggestive glances of the two executioners towards the viewer, which could indicate an invitation to complicity and also a particularly gloating mockery, and secondly the head of an ancient statue, whose significance will be explained. A similar penetrating inclusion of the public by direct eye contact is otherwise only to be found in Velázquez at this time.

Certainly the most impressive depiction of physical torture is visible in Ribera's version of the *Martyrdom of St. Bartholomew* (ill. 32) which is now in the Museu Nacional d'Art de Catalunya in Barcelona. The above-mentioned background figures are present, facing each other and this time acting as some sort of witnesses, although they appear totally indifferent to what is happening (ill. 33).

The version of the *Martyrdom of St. Bartholomew* now in the National Gallery of Art in Washington (ill. 34) points in quite a different direction. As Nicola Spinosa convincingly explains, a kind of human solidarity is created, both between victim and persecutor and between these two and the witnesses in the background. In a society that demanded pain and brutality, all the participants seem to play their parts more or less tranquilly.

In the context of "confessionalization," pictures had an important function as religious propaganda. On the

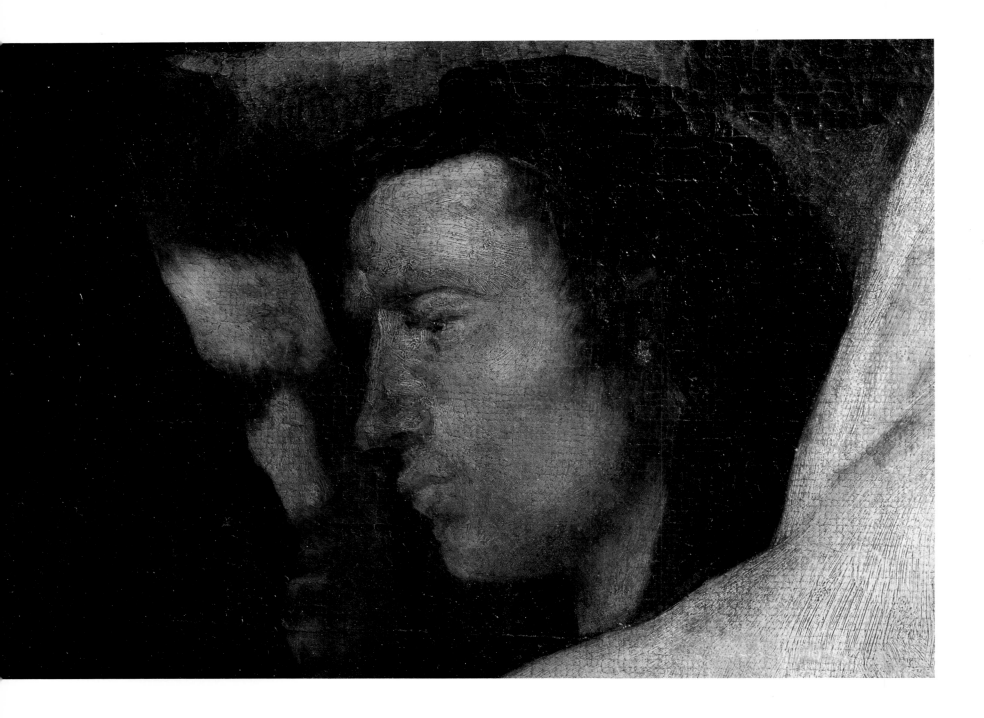

33 Martyrdom of St. Bartholomew (detail of ill. 32)

A characteristic feature of Ribera's pictures are the figures in the second pictorial plane, who are often almost as large as the protagonists in the foreground. They are of course, at best, half-length or partly concealed, and are totally indifferent to the principal event. However, as they are often in dialog with each other, we might think that in the case of St. Bartholomew they are discussing his fate. In this connection, it is interesting to compare the two versions of *Apollo and Marsyas* (ills. 44, 46), where the satyrs that take over the role of the witnesses react in one version with great horror to the flaying of Marsyas and in the other behave entirely passively.

Catholic side saints occupied the foreground, with all national groups able to participate equally. Theirs was an important identifying and integrative role in a society marked by deep social conflict. However, the presentation of cruelty in art can also be explained by recalling that, while Ribera was painting his representations of the *Martyrdom of St. Bartholomew*, the Thirty Years' War was raging between the various confessions in the heart of Europe. Although southern Italy lay far removed from the main theaters of war and its damaging effects, on the Catholic side great efforts were made to deploy the faithful, whether by demanding financial sacrifice from them or conscripting them into the armies. The dramatically depicted images of the saints could therefore supply outstanding models and at the same time help to compensate for the permanent presence of violence in everyday life in the form of numerous public executions and often very

bloody duels. However, to clarify whether Ribera's work really operated in this manner as propaganda, we also need to consider his non-religious depictions of violence as part of the conundrum.

34 *Martyrdom of St. Bartholomew*, 1634
Oil on canvas, 104 x 113 cm
National Gallery of Art, Washington

This work has all the typical features of Ribera's treatment of the subject. The *Marytrdom of St. Bartholomew* shows the confrontation of actor and victim rendered dramatic by the lighting, with indifferent witnesses in the background. And yet it communicates a quite strange message. Executioner and saint appear to play out their roles almost serenely in a society which demands suffering and brutality. In coloration the work also differs from the other versions. The use of color now displays qualities that recall Anthony van Dyck and Venetian painting. The natural lighting illuminates all the details with warm tones.

35 *Martyrdom of St. Bartholomew*, 1628–1630
Oil on canvas, 145 x 216 cm
Galleria Palatina, Palazzo Pitti, Florence

Unlike artists living in Spain, in Naples Ribera had an
opportunity to study buildings and sculptures of antiquity.
Given this, it is surprising how little he introduces features
of classical antiquity into his works, particularly in
comparison with his Italian colleagues. Sculptural heads
are an exception, occurring in several versions of St.
Bartholomew and in the *Allegory of Touch* (ill. 2). In the
martyrdom pictures, the head of Apollo could be a
concealed allusion to the mythological subject of *Apollo
and Marsyas* (ills. 44, 46), which likewise concerns flaying;
an educated public would not have missed this analogy.

36 El Greco and Jorge Manuel Theotokopoulos
Immaculate Conception, c. 1608–1614
Oil on canvas, 108 x 82 cm
Museo Thyssen-Bornemisza, Madrid

This painting of the Immaculate Conception is one of
several in which El Greco treated a subject of much
importance in Spain. His expressive interpretation appears
to anticipate Ribera's innovative pictorial solutions, and
goes far beyond the strictly regulated representational
manner usually seen in the Iberian Peninsula. The
landscape with its symbols of the Virgin in the lower field
has parallels in works by Pacheco (ill. 38). However, it was
probably painted not by El Greco himself but by his son
Jorge Manuel.

The Immaculate Conception is one of Ribera's most
successful subjects. It is not the Immaculate Conception of
Christ (never questioned by Catholicism) but that of the
Virgin, who – according to ecclesiastic dogma – thereby
remains free of all stain of original sin. The declaration of
an appropriate principle was at the time a matter of
dispute between the Spanish Habsburgs and the Papal
Church, and was intensively discussed in Rome between
1610 and 1630.

If we accept the history proposed by Suzanne Stratton,
the concept of an "immaculate conception" of the Virgin
originated in the Greek Church in the 2nd century, and
spread from there to the west during the Middle Ages.
From 1387, two Christian orders were the principal dispu-
tants as to the legitimacy of the idea, with the Dominicans
rejecting the concept and the Franciscans proposing its
elevation to dogma, which was finally effected in 1854.

For the whole period of the dispute, Spanish theologians
played a prominent part. However, it was only in the 17th
century that the new doctrine found wide support in the
Iberian Peninsula among both populace and kings. In
Seville in particular, church feast days and processions on
the subject of the Immaculate Conception induced Philip III
(1598–1621) to summon a group of experts in 1616, the
Real Junta de la Inmaculada Concepción, to set about
persuading the pope. This initiative was followed by many
others by the Spanish.

The cautious attitude of the popes in this matter was to
some extent the result of Protestant criticism, especially of
the Roman practice of canonization. A new commission
had been set up to deal with similar questions in the
Vatican in 1588, and between 1625 and 1634 Urban VIII
(1623–1644) finally reformed the whole system of canonization. A further distinction was made between the *beati*,
the blessed who were candidates for canonization, and
those who were actually canonized. An additional require-
ment was that the candidate should have been deceased
at least 50 years before appropriate proceedings could be
instituted.

The debate about the doctrine of the Immaculate
Conception coincided with the most intensive phase of the
corresponding regulatory reform. Between 1523 and 1588
and again 1629–1658 there were no canonizations at all.
Between 1588 and 1600 there were only two, and in the
whole 17th century only 24 candidates made it.

Pictures were always important in the process of canonization in that they helped a candidate to establish a case.
Though there was a rule that non-canonized persons
should not even feature in portraits, this was enforced only
half-heartedly. One of the most prominent cases of its
being ignored was the campaign on behalf of the founder
of the Jesuit Order, Ignatius Loyola. It owed its success to a
marked extent to the pictorial representations of him and
his deeds. Only following Urban VIII's reforms was such
campaigning strictly forbidden.

The depiction of the Immaculate Conception of the
Virgin, which had enjoyed a degree of popularity even in
the Middle Ages, was not banned even during the
sustained discussion of the doctrine. The debate centered
much more on what the corresponding pictures could and
should show. Interestingly, El Greco, possibly because of
the particular Spanish involvement in the matter, painted
the subject several times (ill. 36). This was remarkable inasmuch as in his native Crete the artist was still Orthodox,
and the Orthodox Church then as now totally rejects the
doctrine of the Immaculate Conception. Although Philip III
himself made the subject of the Immaculate Conception a
personal crusade, it was not until the reign of Philip IV
(1621–1665) that the campaign's greatest successes came.
He managed to get a decree out of Pope Gregory XV
(1621–1623) that went beyond all previous concessions
and banned even private mention of the possibility that
the Virgin herself had been conceived "in sin".

Familiarity with this historical background is essential to
a proper understanding of the importance of Ribera's most
famous version of the *Immaculate Conception*, for the
Count of Monterrey in Salamanca. As ambassador to the
Papal court for Philip IV, the Count had taken up cudgels
for the dogma on his first official journey to Italy, and his
commission of a painting celebrated not only his own
success but also the achievement of his king.

Along with this political and clerical background,
Ribera's own pictorial sources are of interest. Among
these, a distinction should be made between the works of
an older Spanish painting tradition and a new iconography
and style which developed during the debate in Rome. The
former are notable for their pronounced didactic intent, as
can be seen for example in Vicente Macip (1475–1550)
(ill. 37). The fact that the cult had still to be established
required a polemical presentation. For this reason, Macip's
picture, which is of a type called *tota pulchra* dating from
the end of the 15th century, shows the Mother of God
floating over the world with folded hands surrounded by
biblical symbols of purity. These symbols are additionally
furnished with texts and refer to the virginal conception.
Above the Virgin is a representation of the divine trinity
with a scroll, with God the Father and Christ emphasizing
her special position by crowning her. This very wooden
form of representation remained dominant in Spain for a
time, though painters such as Francisco Pacheco (ill. 38)
and his pupils and son-in-law Velázquez endeavored to
instill some life into the subject.

Initially, Pacheco's strict composition seems to recall the
older version by Macip, but Pacheco reduces the symbols
of purity around the Virgin to a halo of stars and the crescent moon. He replaces the others with heads of putti,
which, though they still look stiff, look forward to the
angelic aura essentially woven of light and bodies in Ribera
or Murillo. Other motifs such as the tower and the garden
of Eden are integrated into the landscape in the lower field

38 Francisco Pacheco (baptized 1564–1654)
Immaculate Conception with the poet Miguel Cid, 1621
Oil on canvas, 150 x 109.2 cm
Sacristía de los Cálices, Seville Cathedral

The *Immaculate Conception* by Pacheco displays the strict
composition typical of Spanish tradition, in which the Virgin is
shown standing motionless, surrounded by her attributes or the
heads of putti. There is a coastal landscape, similar to that found in
Ribera later, in which famous Sevillan motifs – the Giralda (the
Moorish tower of the Cathedral) and the Torre de Oro (part of the
Moorish fortifications in the harbor) – are integrated along with
several symbols of the Virgin.

37 (facing page)
Vicente Macip (c. 1475–1550)
Immaculate Conception
Banco Hispano Americano, Madrid

Vicente Macip, one of the most important painters of the Spanish
Renaissance, came from Valencia like Ribera. Several works, such as
the retable in Segorbe Cathedral, were created in collaboration with
his son Juan de Juanes. Earlier the iconography of the *Immaculate
Conception* was also attributed to Juanes, the better known of the two
painters. Since then, an early 16th-century printed engraving has
been identified as the source.

39 Peter Paul Rubens (1577–1640)
Immaculate Conception, 1627
Oil on canvas, 198 x 124 cm
Museo del Prado, Madrid

This picture was a gift by a Spanish nobleman to Philip IV, the great
advocate of the doctrine of *Immaculate Conception*. The Spanish king
had it hung in the chapter houses of the royal palace and monastery
of El Escorial. The iconography is unusual for the subject in the 17th
century and had no influence on subsequent treatments of the
subject in Spain even though the picture was demonstrably accessible
to several artists including Velázquez. Crowned with twelve stars, the
Virgin stands not only on a crescent moon but also on the serpent
with the apple. Two angels flanking her bear the martyrs' bough and
laurel wreath.

40 Alonso Cano
Immaculate Conception, 1655
Cedarwood, height 50 cm
Sacristy, Granada Cathedral

Like Diego Velázquez, Alonso Cano was trained in the workshop of Francisco Pacheco. He worked not only as a painter but also as an architect and sculptor. The small *Immaculate Conception*, which he painted himself, is a Baroque, fully sculpted version of an iconographical subject that features widely in Spain. Although the pose of the Virgin is still very calm in accordance with Spanish tradition, the rich drapery catches the light to striking effect, creating a much more vivid impression than Pacheco's pictures (ill. 38).

in a typically Sevillan way. A unique feature of Pacheco's painting is the insertion of a portrait of the donor Miguel Cid, who wrote a celebrated poem in honor of the *Immaculate Conception* that was set to music and sung in the streets of Seville, again emphasizing the popularity of the Virgin.

Outside Spain, the iconography was handled differently. The numerous symbols of purity were cut back or omitted altogether. Often the depiction features only a crescent moon under the Virgin's feet and an aura of twelve stars around her head, both also symbols of the "woman of the Apocalypse". On the other hand, all the non-Spanish representations of this subject show greater dynamism, either in physical movement or in the Virgin's drapery, and leave more room for the angels glorifying the Virgin. These are the characteristics both of Rubens's version for the Spanish king (ill. 39) and works by Reni and Lanfranco. Of particularly lasting influence were Reni's version of 1627 for the Duke of Alcalá and Lanfranco's painting for the Roman church of the Capuchins dated 1628–1630.

Ribera's achievement was in combining the two traditions, blending Spanish examples with Lanfranco's approach. The result was a simple, skillful solution subsequently much imitated, notably by Murillo, who became famous particularly on the strength of his various versions of this subject. Among Spanish sculptors too a livelier approach ensued, as can be seen in the example by Alonso Cano (ill. 40).

The debate about the *Immaculate Conception* of the Virgin came to a head in Spain, and the iconography finally took on its approved ecclesiastical form there, even though the dogma itself was only formulated in 1854. The artistic guidelines were set out in great detail in Pacheco's treatise on art *Arte de la Pintura* written 1634–1638 and published posthumously in 1649.

Though himself only an average talent as a painter, Pacheco was very influential as a theoretician. He had assembled a circle of distinguished scholars around him in Seville, and several leading artists of the 17th century, including Velázquez and Cano, passed through his workshop. As an expert for the Inquisition, he carried unusual authority. Pacheco's original contribution to Spanish art theory consists mainly in formulating standards for the appropriate iconography of important Christian subject matter by writing an encyclopedic compendium of older, mostly Italian art literature. In the appendix to Part III of his book *Arte de la Pintura*, various Christian subjects are discussed as forms for representation, and well-known artistic examples are cited. A comparison of Ribera's *Immaculate Conception* painted for the Count of Monterrey with the form of representation recommended in Pacheco's standard work reveals both similarities and dissimilarities that testify to Ribera's individual innovative treatment of the subject. Conformity in Ribera is found in

the white tunic with a blue cloak recommended by Pacheco for the Virgin instead of the hitherto normal red tunic such as appears in Velázquez, for example; individuality is evident in Ribera's Virgin's standing on an upturned crescent moon rather than the downturned crescent preferred by the Sevillan writer.

The subject of the *Immaculate Conception* shows that certain questions of faith occasioned controversy not just in the dispute with Protestants and Calvinists but also within the Catholic Church. Factions formed not just around the various orders but also around individual Catholic rulers in Europe. As Peter Burke demonstrates in his essay *How to become a Counter-Reformation Saint*, there were a relatively large number of Spaniards among the few saints to be canonized in the 17th century, not least because Spain exercised the greatest political influence in Europe at the time.

The position of Naples between the Hispanic world and the Church state made it a laboratory for innovation in the Catholic "confessionalization" process, offering Ribera an ideal environment for his artistic development. His influential *Immaculate Conception* is thus as much the result of the particularly open climate prevailing there – which probably enabled him to become familiar with Lanfranco's very recent new version of the *Immaculate Conception* among other things – as of the advocacy of the new cult by the Spanish king and the viceroy, the Count of Monterrey.

CLASSICAL MYTHOLOGY AND VIOLENCE

41 *Ixion*, 1632
Oil on canvas, 301 x 220 cm
Museo del Prado, Madrid

As breaking on the wheel was still customary in the 17th century, it was thought for a time that *Ixion* represented a contemporary scene of punishment. The pointed ear of the executioner does not fit this view, since it makes him unambiguously mythological, a satyr. It is one of the few (and relatively discreet) mythological attributes in the otherwise firmly earthbound pictorial world of Ribera. In contrast to *Tityus* (ill. 42) Ribera chose a portrait format for *Ixion*, although for a time this was considered a landscape format and hung accordingly.

In the past, commentators tended to interpret the not infrequent depictions of violence or latent physical threat from torture or death in Ribera's work as an expression of the artist's own emotional world. In the 19th century, Lord Byron (1788–1824) observed in *Don Juan* that "Spagnoletto tainted/His brush with all the blood of all sainted." Another Romantic writer, the Frenchman Théophile Gautier (1811–1872), considered that Ribera painted things that would make even an executioner recoil with horror. The painter required all his skill and diabolical energy to bear his own violent representation of a flaying, knacker's work that seems to have been carried out for cannibals with the help of an executioner.

These views of Ribera have been attacked in recent times, especially by Spanish writers. They claim to find the same subject matter in the works of Italian artists who, unlike Ribera, are now more or less largely forgotten. They now consider this subject matter, which was previously always attributed to the artist's Spanish origins, as Ribera's individual reaction to the demands of the Council of Trent and a concession to a general change in public taste.

The paintings which were supposed to typify Ribera as a painter of perfidious cruelty were the pictures of the punishment of the damned, Tantalus, Sisyphus, Tityus and Ixion. In 1675, Joachim von Sandrart noted in his art treatise *Teutsche Academie* that Ribera had painted pictures of the punishment of Ixion for the Dutch merchant Lucas van Uffel. The influence of Ixion's painted torment allegedly caused van Uffel's wife to give birth to a child with similarly misshapen fingers: "... [Ixion's] fingers seem to be bent with pain and therefore so terrible that, when this large work of art was set up in her barn in Amsterdam, the wife, Jacoba van Uffel, was at once so unwell that she brought forth her next son to the world with crooked, deformed fingers ..."

The story of Ixion, whose depiction by Ribera had such sinister side effects, is recorded in the *Metamorphoses* (IV, 461) of Ovid (43 B.C. to 18 A.D.). Ixion was punished for murdering a relative and pestering the goddess Hera. He was tortured in the underworld by being chained to a winged wheel which revolved continuously at an alarming speed.

Palomino records that this series of paintings for van Uffel was sent back to Italy as a result of its unfortunate effects. It later passed to the Real Palacio del Buen Retiro in Madrid. This led to the assumption that the paintings were identical to two pictures of *Ixion* (ill. 41) and *Tityus* (ill. 42) now in the Prado. In fact, the history of the paintings is more complicated than that, and the existence of several versions shows once more how popular these extreme depictions of violence were among the contemporary public. Indeed, in 1632, the same year as Ribera painted the series for van Uffel, he did a second series that was sold out of private ownership in 1634 to the royal palace. The Prado versions come from this series. But the pictures from Amsterdam are also documented to the extent that the Prado possesses four studio copies of them. In addition to this, there are written sources which prove the existence of other paintings of giants in Spanish collections. A *Prometheus* that turned up not long ago in the art trade may have belonged to another series. Prometheus and Tityus both suffered the same punishment: they were chained to a rock for eternity while an eagle continuously devoured their livers, their livers always growing back.

This example is particularly illuminating for Ribera's use of depictions of violence. Champions of the theory that Ribera was a thoroughly normal "Italian" painter usually bring up the *Tityus* as an example and compare it to works of Italian contemporaries. In truth these are quite alien to the Spaniard's thinking. This applies not only to the works of Pellegrino Tibaldi (1527–1596) and Ludovico Carracci cited by Pérez Sanchez, but also to the possible model of Titian, whose work could have been known to the Spanish artist through engravings. In 1548, Titian did a series of damned souls for Mary of Hungary, which included a *Tantalus* and a *Tityus*.

The *Tityus* of Titian, likewise in the Prado, is inserted into the frame almost horizontally exactly like Ribera's. But whereas the Venetian painter tells a story in his painting, Ribera makes the viewer *feel* it, thereby arousing curiosity and revulsion simultaneously.

While on the subject of violence, it is noticeable how far Ribera's representations of secular and religious subject matter coincide in this respect. An example shows that, of all the many possible mythological

42 *Tityus*, 1632
Oil on canvas, 227 x 301 cm
Museo del Prado, Madrid

Tityus and Ixion, both transgressors punished by the gods
for their presumption, were conceived as a pair. In the case
of *Tityus* the relationship of picture and frame adds
considerably to the intensification of violence. With the
victim's bound limbs formally crammed into the frame,
every possible escape is cut off optically as well. The
diabolical head of the eagle looms up out of the twilight,
imbuing the whole with an atmosphere more familiar
from the much later *Ghost Stories* of Johann Heinrich
Füssli (1741–1825).

subjects he could have chosen, the artist selected the
one which, as in the case of St. Bartholomew, has a
flaying at the center of the story, namely *Apollo and
Marsyas* (ills. 44, 46). There are also several versions of
this subject. Besides the two surviving versions, which
are both signed and dated 1637, at least two others are
recorded in the written documentation. The basic
story was once again taken from Ovid's *Metamorphoses*:
Marsyas challenged Apollo, the god of the arts, to a
musical duel but was beaten, upon which the god
flayed him for his presumption. In the pictures we see
the torture beginning, with the two protagonists
centrally positioned in front of a tree that rises diagonally to the right. Small differences between the two
versions relate to the presentation of the foreground
and background. In the picture in Brussels (ill. 44) we
see the witnesses (familiar from other works by Ribera)
deep in conversation about the event, whereas in the
Naples version (ill. 46) they watch events horrorstruck.

A study exists for the Naples version (ill. 45). It
shows the protagonists in the final arrangement with
the tree. A graphic work by a contemporary anonymous engraver on the other hand shows Marsyas
already flayed, and Apollo presenting the skin to a
number of warriors. It is thus evident that, in his
painting, Ribera shifts the emphasis away from the
descriptive narrative towards a dramatic elaboration of
the physical torture. The choice of depicting the first
moments of the event allows the artist an opportunity
to heighten the psychological tension between the
torturer and the victim, and to involve the public in
the picture emotionally.

Ribera did of course also paint mythological subjects
that get by without violence. In addition to the
surviving pictures of *Venus and Adonis* (ill. 43) and
Drunken Silenus (ill. 87), we may add those lost in 1734
in a fire at the Alcázar, the old castle and seat of government in Madrid. They included a scene of Bacchus

visiting mortals, of which at least three fragments are preserved in the Prado (ill. 48). A few other pictures are now known only through written documentation.

The multiple depiction of giants and the four versions of *Apollo and Marsyas* compared with the numerous non-violent mythological subjects, of which generally only one version exists, indicates that Ribera's patrons had a pronounced interest in his particularly graphic depictions of violence. This observation is supported by a similar phenomenon with the religious paintings, although the far greater number of pictures makes a global view more difficult. We have already noted the various representations of the *Martyrdom of St. Bartholomew*, whose sufferings, like those of Marsyas, include flaying. Contemporaries seem to have perceived a direct link between the two subjects, the religious and the mythological aspects.

Independently of the earlier version for Osuna, we encounter again and again in Ribera's interpretations a stone head, part of an ancient statue, whose elegant

features suggest an identification with Apollo (ill. 32). With this fragment, an element from an older symbolism, reference is probably being made to the overcoming of antiquity, while a humanistically educated public is simultaneously being addressed via the allusion to the myth of Apollo and Marsyas.

Besides St. Bartholomew's there are other martyrdoms in Ribera's work in which humans are shown being tortured by other humans, such as *St. Philip* (ill. 3), *St. Laurence* and *St. Sebastian* (ill. 29). These subjects appear in the work of other contemporary artists as well, but none of them gives them such quantitative and qualitative weight. Ribera does not just depict barbaric flayings; he includes the feelings of aggressor and victim in the subject, establishing a direct contact between them and the public. Ribera's individual perspective is particularly clear when his pictures are compared with two other examples of extreme violence painted by Poussin (1594–1665) and by Rubens (1577–1640). In the *Martyrdom of St.*

43 *Venus and Adonis*, 1637
Oil on canvas, 179 x 262 cm
Galleria Corsini, Rome

Ribera's depictions of *Venus and Adonis* prove how tricky it could be to paint mythological subjects in the Spanish realm as the 17th century progressed. Even the pro-Enlightenment King Charles III wanted to have all nudes in his royal collection destroyed, including those by Titian. That there were indeed several versions of this subject by Ribera is documented, but only this picture and a questionable attribution have survived. In the present case, the artist quite openly chose a form that could not have offended public decency. Although it still involves a depiction of the goddess of love, Ribera avoids painting indecently naked parts of the body.

44 *Apollo and Marsyas*, 1637
Oil on canvas, 202 x 255 cm
Musées Royaux des Beaux-Arts, Brussels

Instead of an indefinite space steeped in chiaroscuro in the
paintings of the damned (*Tityus, Ixion*, etc.), we find in
Apollo and Marsyas a landscape and figurative painting
whose charm derives from the lightfall from the left.
Equally dominant are the flesh tones of the bodies and the
cooler tones of Apollo's robe, which anticipates the more
strongly classical late work of the artist.

45 *Apollo and Marsyas*, c. 1637
Drawing, pen and brown ink on white paper, 10 x 12 cm
Istituto Nazionale per la Grafica, Rome

This drawing is a preliminary study for the painting in
Naples, as can be recognized from the position of Apollo's
head and the mantle billowing in the wind. Despite the
reduced detail, there are still many motifs from the final
picture: the laurel wreath of the god, the panpipes hanging
in the tree, etc. The position of Marsyas's head and the
violins in the final version nevertheless show that Ribera
made several further changes.

Erasmus, Poussin shows the saint strapped to a torture table, with the executioner gradually removing his intestines with the help of a windlass. In the *Martyrdom of Livinus* (ill. 47) Rubens presents us with a scene in which the tongue just torn out of the saint's mouth is being offered to a dog to eat. The difference from Ribera's pictures lies mainly in the clear references to divine compensation for earthly martyrdom made in both works. Putti descend, proffering the saints palm branches, and heavenly visions promise rewards and atonement at the Last Judgment. There is nothing of this in Ribera; in his pictures, the suffering humans are left alone with their suffering, which makes their situation much worse for them and the viewer. Even the restrained treatment in the depiction of wounds and blood is more a means of intensification than renunciation.

Unlike medieval pictures of violence, the torture now takes place largely in the viewer's imagination, i.e.

there is no exaggerated frenzy to rob the pictures of their gravity. These significant differences were recognized by the Baroque scholar Werner Weisbach in his pioneering work on Baroque as the art of the Counter-Reformation (1921). Weisbach is quoted time and again by the Spanish critics cited earlier in connection with a supposedly stereotypical Ribera picture, but his conclusions are never mentioned: "Ribera's martyrdom pictures are wholly anchored down with the chains of mortality and the impression of suffering. They are among the most somber and gruesome of their kind, devoid of the conciliatory compensation of glory."

It is therefore time to examine more closely the claim that Ribera was reacting to the needs of the contemporary public. Unfortunately there are only a handful of cases where we know the name of the client. Sandrart tells us that the Dutch family van Uffel bought his series of graphic scenes of punishment. Another Dutchman (in fact a Fleming from the southern

46 *Apollo and Marsyas*, 1637
Oil on canvas, 182 x 232 cm
Museo Nazionale di San Martino, Naples

For his treatment of the subject, Ribera chose a moment of transition, which carries powerful psychological conviction. Whereas more graphic depictions often show the flaying completed, here the musical duel between Marsyas and Apollo has only just finished. The musical instruments distributed around the picture – Apollo's violin in the bottom left corner and Marsyas's panpipes, which hang from the branch of a tree like a trophy of victory – are a reminder of it. In the Brussels version, an additional simple flute lies by the head of the tortured loser (ill. 44).

Spanish half of the Netherlands), Gaspar Roomer, had a version of *Apollo and Marsyas* among his seven Ribera paintings. The most important collector in 17th-century Naples, Roomer is described by Francis Haskell in his book about painters and clients during the Italian Baroque as a patron who, like many Flemings fond of the good things in life, had a special taste for grotesque, dark and gruesome things, in short for brutal realism.

If we are to understand why several Netherlanders were among the collectors of Ribera's works and Rembrandt himself (1606–1669) was later among his admirers, we need to bear in mind that, before its exposure to Italian art, the "Spanish school" had been strongly influenced by Dutch models. On the basis of political and economic links, *los reyos catolicos* Isabella I (1451–1504) and Ferdinand II (1452–1516), and later Charles V (1500–1558) and Philip II (1527–1598) as well, had encouraged a lively and intensive cultural transfer from north to south. One of the major roots of Spanish naturalism lay in northern art, and this tradition of a veristic pictorial language was carried by Ribera from Valencia to Rome and Naples. The proximity of his home in Rome to the Dutch artists' quarter is thus also no accident but a deliberate choice of environment that effectively gave expression to a spiritual affinity. We could say with Pérez Sanchez that, in his depictions of violence, Ribera was translating the genre painting developed in the north and its crude features into a "Latin language", in other words a southern idiom that developed out of antiquity.

Although his pictures were clearly well-received by Netherlanders, they were by no means Ribera's only patrons. Like his Dutch colleagues based in Italy, Ribera profited from the Dutch tradition only to the extent that some of his Italian collectors manifested an individual wish for something different from the predominant classical fashion in Italian art. Naples was a city with pronounced social tensions, and violence was an everyday matter. In the Masaniello uprising of 1647/48, the artist stood in grave danger of personally experiencing the violence he had repeatedly painted. Perhaps only his flight into the viceregal palace saved him from injury or worse.

Thus Ribera and some of his artist colleagues incorporated in their pictures the violence they experienced in everyday life, and this was perhaps also a means of learning to come to terms with it. The works of the Spanish artist stand out in that he gives even his mythological and religious figures an earthly context, which repeatedly led to their being wrongly interpreted as representations of contemporary executions and torture. In art treatises, we find artists recommended to take inspiration from contemporary practice in their depictions of martyrdom. And what Caravaggio began, Ribera proved capable of intensifying.

Weisbach sees Ribera's "materialist" painting as incapable of transposing transitory actions into visual terms, considering him the antithesis of Rubens. Yet it is more reasonable to say that Ribera deliberately rejected such propagandist church art. As someone who manifested such great respect for his models, Ribera cannot have been indifferent to the murder going on around him. That the acts of violence become even more prominent in the private world of drawing itself appears to confirm this theory.

Ribera was certainly not a "realistic" painter wanting to express criticism of his time with a supercharged naturalism. Nor yet was he a classical painter – as has been stated occasionally in the literature – who only painted martyrdom so enthusiastically because he liked painting nudes and, given the strict ecclesiastical environment of Naples, this was the only way to do it. What we find in the artist is a sensitive observer of his time who furnishes us with information about the external appearance of his contemporaries as well as about the internal and external tensions they had to live with. This particular perspective fascinated literary figures such as Byron and Gautier in the 19th century, but they themselves "tainted their brushes in blood" too much for us to take their interpretations as art historical analysis.

48 *Head of Bacchus*, c. 1635
Oil on canvas, 55 x 46 cm
Museo del Prado, Madrid

The *Head of Bacchus* is one of three fragments to survive from a larger mythological painting showing the god of wine visiting humanity, which was partly destroyed during a fire at the Madrid Alcázar in 1734. The painting was probably done jointly with a picture by Massimo Stanzione, the *Triumph of Bacchus*, for the vice-regal palace in Naples, after the model of a Hellenistic relief. However, Ribera probably used as his source not the sculptural original known in a number of versions but a printed version dating from 1549. In 1927, art historian August L. Mayer discovered an early copy of Ribera's work, which showed an impression of the whole composition for the first time.

47 (facing page)
Peter Paul Rubens
Martyrdom of Livinus
Oil on canvas, 413 x 347 cm
Musées Royaux des Beaux-Arts, Brussels

The art of Rubens is in many respects an antithesis of Ribera's. Both involve the viewer's emotions in their depictions of a martyrdom, but where Rubens places the whole emphasis on the external pathos, Ribera's focus is on an inner dialog with God. Rubens' picture is full of movement, and the heavenly powers are just as present in it as the earthly torturer. It must have been difficult for the contemporary public to link the scene with their own experiences, which is what the naturalistic pictorial language of Ribera succeeded in achieving.

WORKS FOR THE DUKE OF ALCALÁ – ART THEORY AND BEGGAR PHILOSOPHERS

49 *Magdalena Ventura*, 1631
Oil on canvas, 196 x 127 cm
Hospital de Tavera, Toledo

Among the original artistic touches in this treatment are Ribera's presentation of the woman with her husband and one of her children. It is scarcely conceivable that the protagonists and their child posed as models.
The distribution of gender roles in the pictures and the characterization as a cohesive group instinctively invokes the Holy Family. Only there does the father play such a secondary role, and only there could the artist depict a mother with a bare breast without further ado.
The public of the time must have been very familiar with such classic associations, which must have contributed to the miraculous character of the work and its protagonists.

The patronage of another viceroy, Fernando Enríquez de Ribera, Duque de Alcalá (1570–1637), was of decisive importance for Ribera. Though he was in office only two years, from 1629 to 1631, he was nonetheless an outstanding art connoisseur who had maintained close contacts with Sevillan artists. His stylishly furnished residence of Casa de Pilatos in Seville, the city on the Guadalquivir, can still be visited today, even if the picture it presents of his activities is a reduced one.

On February 11, 1631, the Venetian ambassador wrote home to the Senate that "an outstanding painter is working in the viceroy's rooms on the painting of a woman from the Abruzzi who is married and the mother of numerous children, yet has a wholly male face with a wonderful black beard as broad as a man's hand and a completely hirsute chest. His Excellency had the kindness to show her to me as a thing of wonder, and indeed she is that." This portrait of *Magdalena Ventura* (ill. 49) has survived and can be seen today in the Hospital de Tavera in Toledo. Ribera painted not only the woman but also her husband and one of her children feeding at the breast.

The long Latin inscription on the two-piece stele on the right side of the picture has recently given rise to speculation about Ribera's own theory of art. Freely translated, the text says: "A great miracle of nature, Magdalena Ventura from a town near Accumoli, generally called Samnites, in the Abruzzi in the kingdom of Naples, 52 years old. The amazing thing is that she became very hairy at the age of 37 and began to develop such a long, full beard that she could be taken for a bearded man rather than for a woman who has conceived three sons from her husband Felici de Amici, whom you will find depicted here. Jusepe de Ribera, Spaniard, distinguished with the Cross of Christ, a modern Apelles of his day, painted them at the request of Fernando II, 3rd Duke of Alcalá, Viceroy of Naples, in wonderful fashion from life, on March 14, 1631."

In respect of Ribera's view of art, the most important passages are his ranking himself with the famous painter of Greek antiquity Apelles (375/370 B.C.– 4th century B.C.), *sui temporis alter Apelles*, and the assertion that he not only painted *Magdalena Ventura* from life (*ad vivum*) but also in wonderful fashion (*mire depinxit*). In 17th-century Italy, reality painting, above all life painting from the flesh, was considered by most artists and art theorists as not what art was about, and therefore had a bad reputation. The classical painters who set the tone did not entirely reject working direct from nature, but they demanded that artists take the best elements from various models in order to create an ideal aesthetic work of their own. In 1631, the same year that *Magdalena Ventura* was painted, the main representative of this classicizing school, the painter Domenichino from Bologna (actually Domenico Zampieri, 1581–1641), was on his way to Naples to take over the most prestigious commission in the city at the time, the painting of the Real Cappella del Tesoro di San Gennaro in the cathedral, despite voluble protests from local artists.

Given this background of open conflict between artistic factions, the question arises whether Ribera was quite deliberately making a point with his picture and the inscription, intending to defend his approach to art, so different from the classical style. Indeed, he did not restrict himself simply to making a visual record of the remarkable figure of Magdalena Ventura, but added quite original touches to the painting (ills. 49, 50).

These oddities are clearly intentional, since it states in the inscription that Ribera paints "in wonderful fashion from life." What a purely documentary depiction of the strange phenomenon would have looked like is indicated by the picture of the *Bearded Woman of Peñaranda* by the Spanish painter Juan Sánchez Cotán (1560–1627), which is constantly brought up for comparison. The woman in the picture, Brígida del Río, was taken to the Madrid court in 1590 and painted there by the artist alone and without attributes, in a three-quarter portrait.

Ribera's already prominent equation of himself with Apelles, court painter to Alexander the Great, was a conceit often used at the time by other artists as well, and was intended to trigger certain associations in the viewer. On the one hand, it signaled a confidential relationship between the viceroy and Ribera similar to that traditionally assumed between Alexander and Apelles. On the other hand, this confidentiality – and this could have been particularly important for Ribera – underlined how greatly the artist's style won the

EN MAGNV NATVRA
MIRACVLVM

MAGDALENA VENTVRA EXA
OPPIDO ACVMVLI APVD
SAMNITES VVLGO ELA
BRVZZO REGNI NEAPOLI
TANI ANNORVM 52 ET
QVOD INSOLENS EST CV
ANNVM 37 AGERET COE
PIT PVBESCERE EOQVE
BARBA DEMISSA AC PRO
LIXA EST VT POTIVS

ALICVIVS MAGISTRI BARBATI
ESSE VIDEATVR QVAM MV
LIERIS QVAE TRES FILIOS
ANTE AMISERIT QVOS EX
VIRO SVO FELICE DE AMICI
QVEM ADESSE VIDES HA
BVERAT

IOSEPHVS DERIBERA HIS
PANVS CHRISTI CRVCE
INSIGNITVS SVI TEM
PORIS ALTER APELLES
IVSSV FERDINANDI II
DVCIS III D ALCALA
NEAPOLI PROREGIS AD
VIVVM MIRE DEPINXIT
ANNI M DC XXXI

approval of his client. James Clifton, who has studied the work in great detail, presumes, surely not incorrectly, that the award by the pope of the Order of the Cross of Christ mentioned in the inscription was arranged by the viceroy himself.

Ribera also painted a series of philosophers for the Duke of Alcalá, which possibly included another key work by the artist, the *Democritus* (ill. 54) now in the Prado. This provenance is based only on a reference in the inventory for the Casa de Pilatos in 1637, according to which one of the philosophers shown had compasses as an attribute. However, compasses are a commonly used attribute in Ribera's numerous pictures of scholars, and no reliability can be placed on the provenance.

Signed and dated 1630 on the back of the book in the lower part of the picture, *Democritus* forms one of the beggar philosopher series, so-called because of the subject's dress. During his many travels through the ancient world, the Greek philosopher is supposed to have picked up a wealth of knowledge. Being of a sunny disposition, it caused him to laugh at humanity. His popularity in post-Tridentine art – Ribera's pupil Salvator Rosa (1615–1673) also painted him – is best explained by his philosophy of life, which slipped beautifully into the confessional debate. His idea that people could reach a state of happiness by doing good of their own volition fitted splendidly into the Catholic concept of "free will": a person who committed himself to God in life, acquired the right to a place in heaven. In Protestant doctrine, entry to paradise is by the grace of God.

Another picture of Democritus by Ribera (ill. 52) dates from 1635–1637. Although in both pictures we are confronted with a simply dressed man who provokes us with his cynical laugh, there are nonetheless some important differences. The first picture shows the philosopher standing in a three-quarter length portrait, with compasses as an attribute, while the second presents him as a full-length figure, half-sitting, half-reclining and leafing through a book. On closer study, both works reveal astonishing expressiveness, and we are surely not wrong to assume Ribera's own profession of a certain philosophy of life in them. Even if ultimately it cannot be said with certainty whether the early *Democritus* (ill. 54) formed part of the Duke of Alcalá's collection, it and the portrait of *Magdalena Ventura* (ill. 49) nonetheless convey a supplementary message: in one work, Ribera presents himself as an artist who paints from life "in wonderful fashion;" in the other, he recommends a "pilgrimage" through the real world, which is not just a way to God but also a journey towards the self.

As it was the viceroy and not Ribera who summoned the bearded woman to Naples, it can be presumed that the duke also played a key role in formulating the Latin text in the picture. But specifically what part the duke played in the formulation of any theory of art or even Ribera's philosophy of life is uncertain. With his commissions he was certainly able to steer the Spanish painter in a particular direction. In the case of the inscription, the Duke perhaps helped to put into words what Ribera had already made reality in his artistic oeuvre.

A first decisive shaping of the duke's artistic taste seems to have been at the hands of Francisco Pacheco (the author of *Arte de la Pintura*) and his intellectual acquaintances in Seville. No avowed advocate of naturalism, Pacheco had based his own views largely on classicizing authors and had adopted their aesthetic categories. However, alongside this mainstream orientation of contemporary art theory towards ideal art, Pacheco's exposition shows striking divergences that are clearly due to the example of his own pupil and son-in-law Velázquez. Only thus can we account for Pacheco being less forthright than his Italian colleagues in his criticism of Caravaggio. Moreover, as already mentioned, he treats Caravaggio, Velázquez and Ribera as a separate group.

Unfortunately we have no other artistic background relating to the Duke. A document survives from his time as viceroy of Sicily (1632–1636) giving Ribera instructions for a (now lost) *Mater Dolorosa* commissioned from him, showing the Virgin mourning her son. In this, he touches on both the posture and the desired expression of the figure. In 1636, a year before his death, another naturalistic artist, the Netherlander Pieter van Laer (baptized 1599–after 1642), was able to dedicate to him an eight-part series of prints with representations of sundry animals, which is correctly taken as further evidence of the Duke's interest in genre works.

Finally, the viceroy's very heterogeneous art collection allows us to make inferences about the relationship between Ribera and his patron. In the two surviving inventories, mainly Dutch, Italian and Spanish masters are listed, a combination that is typical of the contemporary art market in Naples and which also shaped Ribera's style.

It includes well-known names such as Guido Reni (1575–1642) and Artemisia Gentileschi (1593–1652/53), but also a series of anonymous artists.

The works of Ribera constitute a marked focal point, but only a copy of Caravaggio's *Madonna of Loreto* (ill. 22), two *bodegones* by Velázquez plus two other works by van Laer can with certainty be attributed to a naturalistic preference.

Of most particular interest are two anonymous pictures of philosophers acquired by the viceroy in 1629, that is before Ribera's pictures. Unfortunately the inventory gives no more detailed information about their composition, and it is thus, an open question whether the figures were already of the beggar-philosopher type that Ribera could have used as a model. Nonetheless, these and other portraits of philosophers in the possession of the duke show that he had a notable interest in the subject. Did he steer Ribera on to the subject and, more especially, did he motivate him into producing the wholly original *Democritus* in Madrid (ill. 54)?

That the Duke of Alcalá was not just another chance client whose patronage was owing to his being in

50 *Magdalena Ventura*, (detail of ill. 49)

Ribera painted the bearded woman from life "in wonderful fashion," which means that he presented what he saw in an artistic interpretation. It is improbable that the family modeled the scene for him like this. Moreover, he places Magdalena Ventura's breast almost in the middle of her upper body, which can hardly have been anatomically appropriate. Probably the artist's intention was to emphasize optically the wonderful presence of the beard by its proximity. Ribera also makes skillful use of the lighting. It can hardly be mere chance that the brightest light reflections are on the child's head, the breast and part of the beard, while the husband (for example) remains in darkness.

51 *Democritus* (detail of ill. 52)

In the various phases of the artist's work we find quite similar figures in shabby clothing but fired from within by self-imposed duties, beginning with the everyday folk of his *Allegories of the Five Senses* (ills. 2, 20, 21, 23) and ending with the *St. Jerome Penitent* (ill. 109) he painted in the year of his death. Yet the special character of these two very different portraits of Democritus lies in the self-conscious laugh. If the self-sufficiency of most Ribera "heroes" is now beyond our understanding, we are quite helpless when it comes to the vital frankness of lives clearly full of privation.

52 *Democritus*, 1635 – 1637
Oil on canvas, 155 x 119 cm
Earl of Pembroke's collection, Wilton House, Salisbury, Wilts

Democritus (460 – 371 B.C.) was one of the most important philosophers of antiquity, though unfortunately only fragments of his writings survive. His strongly materialist and scientific thinking found sympathizers in every century, including Epicurus, Galileo and Leibnitz. In aesthetics, his view was that art should imitate nature. Pictures of him abound mainly in the 17th century.

53 *Preparations for the Crucifixion*, 1628–1630
Oil on canvas, 223 x 174 cm
Parish church of Santa María, Cogolludo (Guadalajara)

Ribera himself noted in a conversation with painter and art connoisseur Jusepe Martínez that his esteem in Spain grew the longer he stayed away from it. In fact, Ribera's works were noted with the greatest interest by artists from his homeland. The influence on Velázquez is relatively clear. Additionally, Jonathan Brown, referring specifically to this picture once in the possession of the Duque de Alcalá, has drawn attention to links with another important master of the *Siglo de Oro*, Alonso Cano. A motif also favored by the latter was the half-concealed figures in the background, very typical of Ribera, and particularly striking in their lack of interest in the events going on in the foreground.

54 (facing page)
Democritus, 1630
Oil on canvas, 125 x 81 cm
Museo del Prado, Madrid

This portrait was long considered a representation of Archimedes because of the compasses and geometrical drawings. But the conspicuous laugh indicates unambiguously the character of Democritus, whom Ribera painted in at least two other paintings. The fictive portrait of the Greek philosopher is also found in the work of his pupil Salvator Rosa. The enigmatic gesture of the scholar is given a subtle setting by the lighting, which reveals itself as the real subject matter of the picture. The head appears as if crowned by the pale gleam of a nimbus.

Naples at the same time as Ribera is indicated by the fact that fairly intensive contacts lasted beyond his relatively short term of office. When ambassador in Rome he had given his predecessor in Naples, the Duke of Alba, a work by Ribera, the *Preparations for the Crucifixion* (ill. 53), and later as viceroy of Sicily he commissioned two works, a graphic work in 1635 and a year later the devotional *Mater Dolorosa* already mentioned. That Luis de Moncada, the Duke of Alcalá's son-in-law, acted as godfather at the baptism of Ribera's daughter may be a further indication of the closeness of their relationship.

According to the art writer Pietro Bellori, the naturalistic painter Ribera also wrested from the viceroy the right to check and correct pictures by the highly regarded classical painter Domenichino before they were sent to Philip IV in Madrid. We may therefore assume that the Duke esteemed his painter and particularly his style. The claim, often made by critics of the naturalistic style, that this kind of painting is mainly suitable for ordinary simple people does not tally with van Laer's dedication to the Duke and the inscription on the picture of *Magdalena Ventura* (ill. 49). Both are in Latin and therefore clearly directed primarily at an educated public.

If we endeavor to sum up the relationship between the Duque de Alcalá and Ribera, i.e. the link between the new Alexander and his Apelles, one particular merit must be acknowledged in the duke. He confirmed the painter's approach to art just as the latter was embarking on the most significant phase of his output. It was not by demanding new iconography but by this confirmation that the Duke was able to steer Ribera in a particular direction. Accordingly, we do not need to seek a putative prototype for the "beggar philosopher" in the viceroy's art collection, since it is already there in the allegorical figures of the Five Senses painted by Ribera in Rome. In the early 1630s, the cobbler's son again openly admitted his humble origins, and it is the awareness of this that feeds the power of conviction in his pictures. Both his portrait of *Magdalena Ventura* (ill. 49) and the *Democritus* (ill. 54) seem true-to-life figures to whom we are willing to accord the same respect as the artist.

Ribera does not confine himself simply to painting what he saw but embraces a certain pictorial tradition at the same time. We have already mentioned Caravaggio's *Supper in Emmaus* as a model for the male *Allegories of the Five Senses* (ills. 2, 20, 21, 23). Another painting by Caravaggio seems to have been relevant for *Democritus*, viz. *St. Jerome* (ill. 16) from the Galleria Borghese. Both paintings show an ascetic scholar who, though characterized by only a few attributes, is presented as a fully developed personality with a natural authority.

The basic differences lie in dress and the relationship with the viewer. Whereas Caravaggio's *St. Jerome* is wrapped in an expensive, gleaming red cloak and is wholly absorbed in his studies, Ribera's *Democritus* wears humble clothes and seeks direct eye contact with the viewer. The comparison of these two works reveals

unmistakably the change in perspective between the 16th and 17th centuries. In place of the withdrawn Father of the Church absorbed in his humanist readings, we have the world-hardened philosopher who looks the viewer and thus reality in the eye and can only laugh at book learning.

We are surely not going too far in seeing quite specific changes in "confessionalization's" choice of media reflected in this change of models. Investigations of reading patterns at the end of the 16th century in Spain show that pictures increasingly began to replace books. The Latin schools so favored under humanism were closed everywhere and, instead, institutions of the Catholic Church began to invest huge sums in the visual furnishings of their churches. Independent reading left too much room for individualist thinking, which was difficult to control. Paintings and statues on the other hand reached a much larger public, which was only too willing to be overwhelmed by splendid settings instead of asking questions. With his "poor but happy" figures, Ribera created new protagonists not just for Catholic confessionalization but also for the Spanish viceroys. The lower classes could identify with them, and aristocratic art collectors could gaze at them like exotic flora. But over and above this Ribera puts a pictorial message into his depiction of beggar figures that can trouble us even today. What does all wealth or all knowledge profit us if a "poor" man comes and laughs at it (ill. 51)?

Noise, crowds of people and, for the time, unusually tall houses of four to six stories were the principal impressions that must have first struck visitors to Naples in the 17th century (ill. 55). This is confirmed by Giulio Cesare Capaccio: "I see so many people in every street, in every alley and at every street corner who bump into me and trample me underfoot, and I find it difficult to get out of their way; ... I go into the churches, which are numerous, and find them full of people; people are everywhere outside, too, if we're not to overlook those who are at work, at home or in offices and other buildings; you see streets full of people – pedestrians, riders or in carriages – not one street or ten, but all of them."

The reason for the great throng was the relatively small land area of the city, home in the mid-17th century to around 360,000–370,000 people. It was a population that ranked Naples second among European cities (ill. 56). Numbers had been rising rapidly since the 16th century, because difficult living conditions in the country drove people into the cities. Only in Naples could they escape the repressive hand of the large landowners and constant threat from bandits. Additionally, urban dwellers were generally free from most taxes, could obtain food cheaply and, initially at least, found work easily. There was paid work for simple laborers in the textile trade, construction

and in all industries connected with the sea. Work related to government, trade and banking offered occupations with social prestige.

Society was organized on strictly hierarchical lines. Capaccio describes two categories, the nobility and the people (*popolo*), with the latter divided into burghers and plebeians. The city government was conducted by an assembly that included five members representing about 130 aristocratic families and an appointed representative of the burghers; the latter was selected by the viceroy from six candidates. The plebeian classes, who had no representative of their own in the administration, comprised very diverse social groups. There were artisans and shop-owners, but also *lazzaroni* or beggars, who eked out their living by providing small services or through petty crime. The term *lazzaroni* dates from Ribera's day, when the beggars first constituted an identifiable social group. Painters, although still artisans in Spanish terms, were grouped with printers, goldsmiths and architects among the burghers.

The origins of Spanish rule in southern Italy go back to 1282, when Peter III of Aragón seized Sicily. In 1443, Alfonso V (1416–1458), likewise Aragonese, was additionally granted the fiefdom of Naples by the pope. By Ribera's time, however, there were once again separate viceroys for the two territories (ill. 58). The Spanish Habsburgs broke

55 Didier Barra
Bird's eye view of Naples, 1647
Oil on canvas, 69 x 129 cm
Museo Nazionale di San Martino, Naples

Didier Barra was born in Metz, France. From the 1630s to the end of the 1650s (that is, during the last phase of Ribera's life), he worked in Naples as a producer of *vedute*. His oeuvre is reconstructed from the relatively few works that can be definitely attributed to him. One of them is this prospect of Naples, which is signed and dated. This picture demonstrates Barra's skill in giving a very individual, painterly interpretation without sacrificing topographical accuracy.

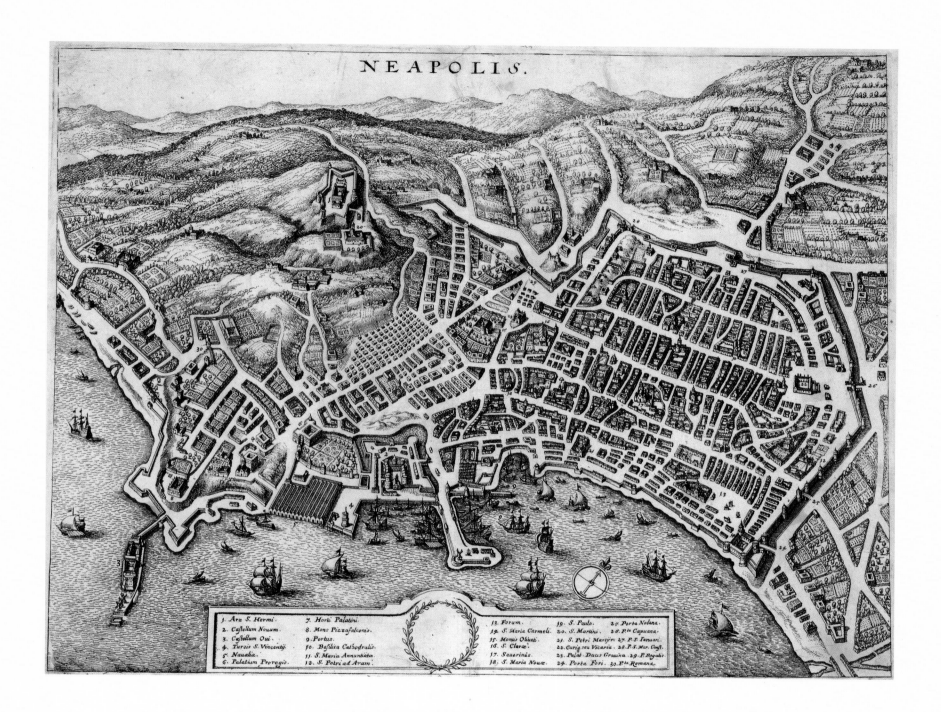

1. Arx S. Hermi.
2. Castellum Nouum.
3. Castellum Oui.
4. Turris S. Vincentij.
5. Naualia.
6. Palatium Proregis.
7. Horti Palatini.
8. Mons Pizzofalconis.
9. Portus.
10. Basilica Cathedralis.
11. S. Maria Annunciata.
12. S. Petri ad Aram.
13. Forum.
14. S. Maria Carmeli.
15. Monis Oliueti.
16. S. Clarae.
17. Seuerinus.
18. S. Maria Nouae.
19. S. Paulo.
20. S. Martini.
21. S. Petri Martyr.
22. Curia seu Vicaria.
23. Palat. Ducis Grauina.
24. Porta Fori.
25. Porta Nolana.
26. P.ta Capuana.
27. P. S. Ianuari.
28. P. S. Mar. Cost.
29. P. Regalis.
30. P.ta Romana.

the power of the great aristocratic families in the viceroyalty of Naples by forcing them to leave their country seats and put themselves under the control of the court in the capital. Indeed, some of the Spanish viceroys in the early 17th century would have liked to go further by limiting the political dominance of the nobility in the governing committees. With the aim of undertaking major reforms, these Spaniards co-operated with sections of the local opposition, which included a number of intellectuals such as the philosopher Tommaso Campanella (1568–1639), who wrote the famous utopian work *The Sun State*. Enrique de Guzmán, the Duke of Olivares, who was

viceroy of Naples from 1595–1599, failed to push his reforms through. Pedro Fernández de Castro, Duke of Lemos, who restricted himself to administrative and financial reforms in his term of office from 1610–1616, had more success. He was particularly keen to reinforce the exchange with Spain and to strengthen the presence of Spanish culture in Naples. With this in mind, he not only carried out the reorganization of the university on the lines of the famous Spanish institution in Salamanca but also supported the important cultural body of the Accademia degli Oziosi, which included adherents of the Neapolitan reform movement. The most progress was made by the

56 *Map of Naples*, 1646
from: Pierre d'Avity "Newe archontologia cosmica"
Wolfgang Hoffmans Buchtruckery, Frankfurt am Mayn
New York Public Library, New York

Before the plague of 1656 Naples was very densely populated. In the west were the palaces of the upper classes and the important government buildings including the viceroy's palace, where Ribera took refuge during the Masaniello uprising. In the east was the poorer district and also the cathedral. The center of unrest in 1647/48 was around the parish church of Santa Maria del Carmine and the modern Piazza del Mercato.

D. Pietro Giron Duca d'Ossuna Iuniore Vicere luog.te e Capt.n Gente, nel Regno di Nap. anno 1616

T.II. P. 87.

57 Duque de Osuna, 1692
from: Parrino, "Teatro eroico de' Vicere di Napoli"
Bayerische Staatsbibliothek, Munich

The portraits of the viceroys are included in the "Teatro eroico de' Vicere di Napoli," published by Parrino in 1692. When Ribera arrived in Naples in 1616, the Duke of Osuna's term of office was just beginning. The duke was particularly keen to reform the political structures of Naples, and was supported in this by local opposition to the ruling aristocracy. These efforts cost him his office and his liberty, but the failure to implement them was one cause of the Masaniello uprising in 1647/48.

Duke of Osuna (in office 1616–1620), Ribera's first important patron in the city (ill. 57). He adopted one of the main demands of the opposition, that of equal representation of nobility and burghers in the city government, and worked with the lawyer Giulio Genoino, who led a broad popular movement. But the government in Madrid under the ostentatiously pious Philip III opposed all changes, relieved the Duke of Osuna of office and had Genoino incarcerated in a North African fortress.

Whereas nobility and burghers had been political adversaries in the conflict of 1620, the protagonists in the Masaniello uprising were initially the plebeians, especially the *lazzaroni*. However, it is presumed that Genoino was once again significantly involved behind the scenes. When the revolt broke out on July 7, 1647, the direct causes were famine, high food prices and rising taxes. The high duties on wheat, fruit and vegetables, which were intended to fund Spanish participation in the Thirty Years' War, hit the population particularly hard (ill. 59).

Most interpretations of the uprising describe it as the result of blind mass fury in which the people reacted to external circumstances without developing individual characteristics or even an organized movement. This assessment is based on contemporary reports, which of course include no statements from the rebel side. However, historian Peter Burke sees a ritualized sequence of events, especially from the ten-day period at the beginning of the unrest to the murder of the revolutionary leader Masaniello on July 16. This view is of interest in lending the *lazzaroni* a character of their own, and may help us to understand why Ribera devoted so much attention to this social group in his pictures. Because both his beggar philosophers and the final version of *Maria Aegyptica* of 1651 are clearly stamped with the markers of the *lazzaroni* in their impoverished dress.

According to Burke, the rituals of the revolt – the protest march to the viceroy's palace with loaves on spears, the "disciplined" looting of the financiers' palaces, the "orderly" forms of vengeance, justice, etc. – were aimed at strengthening the cohesion of the rebels and at the same time giving them an effective outlet. The results of his research indicate that the protests were sustained not

58 *Political divisions of Italy in 17th century*
from "Italiæ novissima descriptio auctore Jacobo Castaldo Pedemontano"
Libreria di Città, Naples

In the 17th century, modern Italy was divided into many political units. Large parts of it belonged for a time to the Hispanic World or were dependencies of it like the viceroyalties of Naples and Sicily and the city states of Milan and Florence. Also of territorial importance were Venice and the Papal State, to which Bologna (among others) also belonged.

59 Domenico Gargiulo
The Masaniello Uprising, 1656–1658
Oil on canvas, 126 x 177 cm
Museo Nazionale di San Martino, Naples

According to Dietrich Erben, this picture is presumed to
have been painted as part of a group of three history
pictures, which include the eruption of Vesuvius in 1631
and the outbreak of plague of 1656 (ill. 11). The client
was possibly one of the nobles in the city government
during the plague year, whose outlook is reflected here.
Masaniello appears as a mounted figure in the foreground,
although at the historical moment when the heads of the
Spanish sympathizers were publicly presented in the
market place he was already dead.

by a rootless mob but by the poor who were concentrated into certain districts of Naples, above all the *lazzaroni*. A further point in his analysis is particularly interesting here. The rebels were remarkably united in honoring the Virgin, whose representation in a picture in the parish church of Santa Maria del Carmine clearly acted as a powerful symbol of communality. The picture became almost an expression of social identity. What, we may ask, was Ribera's role in this "pictorial conflict"? Did he adopt ideas for his works from "the underdogs", or did he put his work at the service of those who sought to discipline the populace from above?

The special role of the *lazzaroni* in Naples did not end with Don Juan José de Austria's defeat of the revolt in March 1648 (ill. 60). In the 18th century, the ruling Bourbons formed an alliance with the plebeian classes and thus the "complicity" between rulers and the lower classes, which had been discernible in Ribera's paintings of the beggar philosophers for the viceroy, became a reality.

An expression of this unusual 18th-century alliance was King Ferdinand IV's (1751–1825) nickname, *re lazzarone*. This time, the king and the *lazzaroni* were fighting not for better conditions for the latter but against Neapolitan disciples of the Enlightenment, who in 1799 succeeded in gaining control of the city for a few months with the help of Napoleon's troops.

Were Ribera's demonstrations of respect for the poor and marginalized likewise reactionary? We cannot make this automatic assumption, as the situation in Naples in Ribera's lifetime was very different from the political situation in the 18th century. Yet we cannot overlook that even in the 17th century representations of poverty took on quite different features. Along with these respectful depictions, there is in the late Ribera a kind of folksy view of simple people such as the Bamboccianti in particular had popularized in Rome. In Naples, this fashion found its greatest expression in the highly popular figures of cripples, in which not just biblical figures but soon typical figures of southern Italy were depicted, like the macaroni eaters. Further investigation is necessary to clarify the painter's view of the *lazzaroni*.

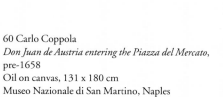

60 Carlo Coppola
Don Juan de Austria entering the Piazza del Mercato, pre-1658
Oil on canvas, 131 x 180 cm
Museo Nazionale di San Martino, Naples

This picture by Coppola depicts the victor over the Masaniello uprising, Don Juan José de Austria, at the head of a large troop of mounted men, accepting the city keys of Naples from a kneeling patrician. The gesture symbolizes the subjugation of the troubles. Dietrich Erben draws attention to the strict arrangement of the pictorial events, and especially the representation of the Archangel Michael above the scene, intended to provide stark emphasis to contemporaries of the legitimacy of the Spanish viceroyalty.

WORKS FOR THE COUNT OF MONTERREY – A CHANGE OF STYLE

61 Bartolomé Esteban Murillo
La Inmaculada de Soult, c. 1678
Oil on canvas, 274 x 190 cm
Museo del Prado, Madrid

Ribera made a vital contribution to developing a new iconography to replace the traditional Spanish *Immaculate Conception*. Whereas the older painter integrated the once-dominant symbols of virginity common in earlier Spanish representations into the composition, thus reducing their optical conspicuousness, Murillo now dispensed entirely with all except the crescent moon in favor of a much more compelling atmospheric setting.

62 *Immaculate Conception*, 1635
Oil on canvas, 502 x 329 cm
Iglesia del Convento de las Agustinas Recoletas de Monterrey, Salamanca

The Virgin Mary stands centrally on a crescent moon. Underneath is an expansive landscape, beneath a broad band of cloud containing numerous putti and two angels rising diagonally from the corners. Top left, over the head of the Virgin, is the half-length figure of God the Father, with the dove of the Holy Ghost.

Don Manuel Fonseca y Zúñiga, the Conde de Monterrey, was in office in Naples as viceroy from 1631 to 1637. This was a period when the renewal of war with the Netherlands demanded severe sacrifices from the Spanish territories in southern Italy, above all in taxes and soldiers. The Spanish Habsburgs no longer sought the support of the reformers as they had in the first decades of the 17th century but collaborated with the large landowners to plunder the region. This led to growing unrest, which culminated in the revolt of July 1647.

Before his spell as viceroy in Naples, the Count of Monterrey had fronted the Spanish embassy in Rome. There too he bought works both for his own collection and for Philip IV, who had built himself a new summer palace whose splendor lay mainly in its rich stock of paintings. Although the artistic taste of Fonseca y Zúñiga was undoubtedly molded largely by the prevailing classicizing Baroque of Gianlorenzo Bernini (1598–1680) or Domenichino in the papal city, he also patronized the continuing naturalistic orientation of Ribera. In view of the works he bought from him and the other works that Ribera produced in these years, it is difficult to avoid the impression that the painter changed his style once again under the influence of his patron, taking account of his Roman preferences. The result was a style more strongly dominated by light and color, such as commonly prevailed in Rome at that time.

The Count of Monterrey possessed the greatest number of pictures by Ribera, but unfortunately the documentation of the commissioning is inadequate. We are thus left to speculate on the exact nature of his patronage. Two groups of works from the time of his connection with Ribera merit particular attention. The first comprises two pairs of apostles. The *St. Roch* (ill. 64) and *St. James the Great* were painted in the early Monterrey period and *St. Peter* (ill. 63) and *St. Paul* in the late Monterrey period. The latter are recorded in an inventory of the Count's art collection in 1653. In each case, they are monumental full-length portraits, with the figures endowed only with their most important attributes.

The second group is connected with the commission for the design of a retable in the burial chapel of the Monterreys in Salamanca. Along with the main picture, the *Immaculate Conception* (ill. 62), which will be discussed elsewhere, Ribera also painted a *St. Januarius in Glory* (ill. 66), which in formal respects displays quite striking parallels to two other pictures, a representation of the *Trinity* (ill. 67) and the *Translation of Mary Magdalene* (ill. 65). All three pictures show the holy figure above a slightly diagonal base of clouds populated by putti, creating a dynamic axis of motion towards the upper right. In two cases, the *St. Januarius in Glory* and *Translation of Mary Magdalene*, we get a bird's-eye view of a landscape in the lower part. We also find expensive drapery blowing in the wind, both in the saints and in the picture of the *Trinity*.

It has already been noted that in 1632 Ribera's style changed markedly with the picture of *Jacob and Laban's Flock* (ill. 18). Although he continued to stick to his basically naturalistic position, he abandoned the contrast-rich chiaroscuro of Caravaggio in favor of a differentiated treatment of light. His new treatment of color is central to this. Ribera not only considerably extended his palette but achieved notable chromatic effects by the transparent application of individual layers of paint. The bodies of his figures now seem to glow from within, and his landscapes are filled with an atmosphere of brilliance.

These are the very elements we find in the two groups of paintings created during his association with the Count of Monterrey. The changes become especially clear if we contrast the two pairs of apostles. They represent Ribera's position before and after the change of style. *St. Roch* (ill. 64) is characterized by the contrast between the harsh brightness of the flesh tones and the dark clothing, on a brown background enlivened only by shadow. This picture is thus still wholly conceived in the tradition of Caravaggio.

St. Peter (ill. 63) on the other hand represents the new style, where flesh tones and clothing are both imbued with light, and the blue background enlivened with silver clouds generates a Mediterranean ambiance.

What prompted this change of style in Ribera? Was it the rediscovery of the atmospheric painting of the Venetians or the example of the Flemish painters Anthony van Dyck and Peter Paul Rubens, two phenomena that agitated artists throughout Italy at the

63 *St. Peter*, 1637
Oil on canvas, 205 x 112 cm
Museo de Bellas Artes de Alava, Vitoria

The portraits of *St. Peter* and *St. Paul* must have been among the last commissions placed with Ribera by the Conde de Monterrey. A preliminary study in the typical pen style of Ribera showing just a few essential features already contains the saint's pose seen in the painting, though the figure in the study, in part due to the medium and in part to the still visible second leg, looks far less animated than the final version, which clearly aims at monumentality. Here, Peter and the large block of stone beside him appear as two aspects of the same idea. This picture is justly compared with works by Zurbarán, whose saints often have a similarly statuesque character. The difference is in the coloration, the detail and above all the very free treatment of the face in Ribera. In comparison with the picture of *St. Roch* some years earlier (ill. 64), the flesh tones and drapery are imbued with light in *St. Peter* and are decidedly colorful, against a blue sky enlivened with silvery clouds. In contrast with the monumentality of the overall figure, the treatment of the beard shows an astonishingly free brush technique and a great variety of light and shade.

64 (facing page)
St. Roch, 1631
Oil on canvas, 212 x 144 cm
Museo del Prado, Madrid

In his different periods, Ribera painted series of apostles of philosophers over and again. Works of this kind are therefore particularly helpful in tracing phases in the artist's development. *St. Roch* with its brownish background structured entirely in shadow, is still cast entirely in the Caravaggesque chiaroscuro mold.

66 *St. Januarius in Glory*, c 1636
Oil on canvas, 276 x 199 cm
Church of the Convento de las Agustinas Recoletas de
Monterrey, Salamanca

This picture was commissioned by the Conde de
Monterrey as a reaction to the eruption of Vesuvius in
1631, which he himself had experienced. This is why the
narrow strip of landscape at the bottom shows a prospect
of Naples, including some of its more notable buildings,
plus the volcano in the background. In this respect, it is
interesting to compare it with the architectural symbol
of Naples in the equestrian portrait of *Don Juan José de
Austria* (ill. 68). The picture of St. Januarius, which was
intended for Salamanca, was painted in Naples and served
there as a prototype for various local artists who
subsequently treated the same subject.

67 *Trinity*, c. 1635/36
Oil on canvas, 226 x 118 cm
Museo del Prado, Madrid

This picture, like the *St. Januarius in Glory* (ill. 66) and the
Translation of Mary Magdalene (ill. 65), is thought to have
been commissioned by the Count of Monterrey. All three
paintings are not just examples of the new, light-imbued
period post-1632, but also share certain features in the
composition. They show the saints above a slightly
diagonal cloud base populated by putti, creating a
dynamic movement to the upper right. The rich wind-
blown drapery of God the Father is also found in the
representation of the *Translation of Mary Magdalene*.

65 (facing page)
Translation of Mary Magdalene, 1636
Oil on canvas, 256 x 193 cm
Museo de la Real Academia de Bellas Artes de San
Fernando, Madrid

The depiction of Mary Magdalene has features in
common with a whole series of paintings by Ribera from
this time. The bird's eye view landscape emphasizes his
interest in this new genre, which preoccupied a number
of artists of the day in Rome.

time by introducing a new concept of light. Undoubtedly it was a combination of several factors. Not the least influential must have been the competition vis-à-vis his Roman colleagues. They had absorbed the many innovations especially quickly and had long enjoyed precedence in Naples, especially among financial institutions, despite the abundance of local talent. For Ribera, the arrival in Naples of a viceroy coming direct from the papal city at this time may have acted as an important catalyst.

But it would be far too simplistic simply to emphasize the link with Rome. Because, just as the Duke of Alcalá formed an important link between Ribera and Velázquez that possibly provided a common basis for both painters' interest in combining elements of genre painting with mythology and religious art, a link can also be established with Spain in respect of the Monterrey paintings. The literature rightly compares Ribera's *Immaculate Conceptions* (ill. 62) with those of Murillo, and the monumental apostle pictures with works by Francisco de Zurbarán (1598–1664), the *Trinity* with that of El Greco (1541–1614), and the *Translation of Mary Magdalene* with a corresponding picture by Claudio Coello (1642–1693).

The fact is that with the commissions from the Count of Monterrey or his entourage Ribera strengthened his position in Naples and exercised a particularly lasting influence. To mention just two Italian artists who took their bearings from him, Andrea Vaccaro (1604–1670) directly borrowed his depiction of *St. Januarius in Glory*, and Luca Giordano (1634–1705) followed Ribera in his versions of the Apollo and Marsyas theme.

Ribera's influence on Neapolitan painting has undoubtedly been long underestimated. If he had not come to the city in 1616, the fire of naturalism fanned by Caravaggio would have been quickly extinguished. But of almost greater significance was his decision to change styles again in the early 1630s. In making himself the protagonist of a new style in the city, he took the wind out of critics' sails and was able to create enthusiasm for his approach among Neapolitan painters, not just among the former Caravaggian school but also in the next generation. In this way, he prevented the polarization of classical painters and naturalists which had typified Rome, and at the same created an individual face for a regional school of painting.

These merits of Ribera were later obfuscated by Italian art writers such as Bellori or his Neapolitan counterpart de Dominici, who sought to understand the situation in Naples in terms of conditions in Rome. Ribera now appeared like Caravaggio as the representative of a false naturalistic approach, contrasted with the light-filled figures of Guido Reni or Domenichino. The Spanish artist was an absolute opponent of Domenichino, but with other representatives of Roman classical painting, notably Reni and Lanfranco, he seems to have found definite points of contact. Bellori's tale of Ribera being after Domenichino's blood during his spell in Naples seems highly unlikely given that, though Ribera was originally an outsider, he had become thoroughly integrated in the city's artistic life, whereas Domenichino was essentially a loner who was reputed to be excessively intolerant. Thus Ribera represented a stroke of luck for Naples, and the far-reaching importance of his work is not least evident in his highly successful pupils, like the Luca Giordano mentioned earlier.

The important role of the three viceroys, the Duke of Osuna, the Duke of Alcalá and the Count of Monterrey, for Ribera's artistic development is also indirectly confirmed by the very few works inspired by political dignitaries in his final years. As Ribera never enjoyed the position of official court painter, his connection with the viceroys had never been institutionalized, but always depended on the individual initiative of the current Spanish representative in Naples. His principal clients now became Church institutions, and this was not without effect on his art.

For Duke Medina de las Torres, who was viceroy from 1637 to 1644, only one outstanding work was created, viz. *The Boy with the Club Foot* (ill. 85). During the Duke of Arcos's term of office (1645–1647) Ribera's illness and the political confusions of the Masaniello uprising prevented the continuation of the once so fruitful patronage. Not a single work can be proved to have been commissioned by the viceroy during this period. However, Don Juan José de Austria, who was dispatched to Naples to quell the uprising and was only in office until March 1648, commissioned a major equestrian portrait (ill. 68). This commission and the closer relationship with this ruler came about in part because Ribera and his family had to seek refuge in the viceregal palace. A relative of the painter was also accused of a love affair with Don Juan José de Austria. The last viceroy in Ribera's lifetime, the Count of Oñate (in office 1648–1653), offered no significant patronage to either Ribera or any other artists.

68 *Don Juan José de Austria*, 1648
Oil on canvas, 319 x 251 cm
Palacio Real, Madrid

This equestrian portrait of Don Juan José de Austria, which was painted in celebration of his successful defeat of the Masaniello uprising, displays numerous links with works in the same genre by Velázquez. Here the parallels are probably accidental, deriving perhaps from a common printed source. The brightly lit background landscape is particularly charming, and rather reminiscent of the Bay of Naples. The etching done by Ribera from the painting (ill. 119) is more explicitly detailed in its depiction of Naples harbor.

THE UNKNOWN RIBERA –
HIS LANDSCAPES

69 *Landscape with fortress*, 1639
Oil on canvas, 127 x 269 cm
Palacio de Monterrey, Salamanca

The clump of trees on the left and the tree stump are *repoussoir* motifs, which became more widely used only in the 18th century. They are there to direct the viewer's eye into the distance. Linked in the foreground by a dark strip, they formed an ideal frame for the bright background landscape. The architectural ensemble on the left edge of the picture appears to be completely integrated into nature and is not, as would have happened in a Roman landscape scene, monumentalized as a reminder of the heritage of antiquity.

70 *Don Juan José de Austria* (detail, ill. 68)

In the background landscape of this equestrian portrait is a high plateau with a massive fortress furnished with corner towers. With the bright light on its walls, it looks like a vision. In the context of the representation of the victorious commander Don Juan José de Austria, fresh from his defeat of the rebels in Naples, this is probably an allusion to the Spanish citadel in the city, Castel Sant' Elmo, which can be seen here in the picture as a symbol of the steadfastness and inevitability of Spanish rule. The Bay of Naples was quite clearly Ribera's topographical model, though he changed the view by deleting the city and Vesuvius. He probably undertook a similar abstraction in the service of a pictorial idea in other paintings, not just in his landscapes.

Landscape elements appear even in the early pictures of Ribera, as for example in the view through the window in the *Allegory of Sight* (ill. 20). But in the 1630s the painter's interest in the subject clearly quickened. It was already known from contemporary sources that Ribera had painted pure landscapes, yet there was general amazement when two such works were recently found in the private ownership of the Alba family.

One shows a coastal landscape with a fortress and fishermen, the other a pastoral group and two boats integrated into the landscape. In both cases they clearly involve ideal landscapes, i.e. landscapes for which no specific geographical model can be found. However, once you know the coastal region of Naples, the artist's specific observations of landscape become directly perceptible. Just as the *Campagna Romana* can be detected over and again the barren landscapes of Poussin, for example in his *Landscape with St. Matthew and the Angel*, in the two paintings by Ribera we encounter the Gulf of Naples.

Ribera's contribution to pure landscape painting dates from 1639, and has to be considered in the context of Roman landscape painting. Though the genre had been considered until then the special domain of the Dutch painters, artists such as Claude Lorrain (1600–1682) and Nicolas Poussin (1594–1665) soon established a leading role for Roman landscape painting. Ribera succeeded in combining the atmospheric mood of landscapes by Lorrain and Poussin with unusual perspectives and original motifs.

In the artist's homeland of Spain, however, landscape painting as such hardly existed before the 19th century. Among the rare exceptions are two prospects of the gardens of the Villa Medici by Velázquez, who painted them on his second stay in Rome in 1649/50. Among the few Spanish oeuvres available for comparison are the works of Francisco Collantes (1599–1656), who is considered by some writers to have been influenced by Ribera.

Ribera's *Landscape with Fortress* (ill. 69) is amazingly harmonious. Conversely, the *Landscape with Shepherds* (ill. 71) captivates with its alternation of shadow and strongly illuminated areas. We see the shepherd on a knoll with a few animals. A comparison of this subject, which was so popular in Roman landscape painting,

with a contemporary picture such as Poussin's *Tranquillity* of 1651 (ill. 72) gives us an idea of the special characteristics of Ribera's style. In the first place, it is noticeable that it involves not a single figure but a pair; this makes identification more difficult for the viewer. Secondly, the group lacks the idyllic quality normally so typical of the subject. The bizarre growth of the trees, their meager foliage, the sandy soil, which is almost a wilderness, the weatherproof clothing suggesting a chill wind (which the clouds confirm), are all in sharp contrast to the transfigured yearning for a secluded life harmoniously at one with nature which is commonly found in contemporary pastoral literature.

From the late 1630s, we frequently find panoramic views in Ribera's figurative works. Here he repeatedly adopts a bird's eye perspective, which is very uncommon for the time. Examples include the *Translation of Mary Magdalene* (ill. 65), *St. Januarius in Glory* (ill. 66), and the equestrian portrait of *Don Juan José de Austria* (ill. 68); or he uses a low horizon, as in the *Boy with a Club Foot* (ill. 85). His pictures increasingly contain depictions of natural elements.

Out of this group of works, which are notable for their balanced presentation of figures and landscape features, sometimes giving them equal status, the picture of *Jacob's Dream* (ill. 73) merits more detailed examination. The painting depicts a subject often represented in Baroque art, i.e. the ladder leading to heaven that Jacob sees in his dream, at the top of which is God speaking of the Promised Land (Genesis 28, 10–22). But unlike other interpretors, Ribera neither includes the usual three-dimensional ladder nor evokes the visionary scene so popular in Spanish paintings, which depict visions seen only in the mind with the utmost realism of detail.

Nature is shown in just a few elements. Jacob's body lies on bare sandy soil, with his head resting on a stone, as the Bible recounts. But the place is lent a special character by the elliptical froaming of part of the surface by a diagonal shaft of light. The edge is marked by two objects: a flat stone and the stump of a tree, placed on a diagonal diametrically opposed to that of the protagonist. Although this work was in the company of another work by Ribera, it is interesting that in the 18th century it was considered to be by

71 *Landscape with shepherds*, 1639
Oil on canvas, 128 x 269 cm
Palacio de Monterrey, Salamanca

The latest discovery of two pure landscapes by Ribera in a private Spanish collection has finally provided concrete knowledge of a facet of his work that hitherto had only been known through documents and the marginal scenes in figurative works. The example of the background landscape in the equestrian portrait of *Don Juan José de Austria* (ill. 68) shows that Ribera drew upon real impressions but then treated them quite originally.

72 Nicolas Poussin
Tranquillity, 1651
Oil on canvas, 97 x 131.5 cm
The J. Paul Getty Museum, Los Angeles

Poussin and Claude Lorrain were the artists who established a new school of landscape painting in Rome using motifs of antiquity. Like Ribera, they drew attention to their own environment, choosing specific reference points in the monument-rich landscape of the Campagna Romana. In content, the present picture is a counterpart to a work called *Storm*, dating from the same time. Compared with Ribera, the first noticeable difference is the much higher horizon. Another important feature is the deliberate contrast between the idyllic landscape and the strictly cubic architectural elements, which introduce a rhythmic articulation into the picture.

Murillo. The Seville artist was particularly in vogue at the time, and unlike Ribera was seen as the painter of light and visions, the very features Ribera adopted in the 1630s. Thus *Jacob's Dream* is proof of the extraordinary range of Ribera's painting and the artist's ability to change. But it is not typical of his late work, and therefore cannot be used as evidence to counter the image of Ribera as a painter of gruesomenesses and ascetic saints, as has recently been attempted.

Yet one basic conclusion can be drawn from the design of the work: there is a similarity in the view of nature and landscape here and Ribera's treatment of figures. The particular power of his pictures results from his restricting them to the essential features of the subject, which was intensified from the mid-1630s by a great delight in color and a different approach to lighting. In respect of composition and individual subjects he repeatedly came up with new and original treatments, but once he found a convincing form – such as the stump of a tree or blocks of stone – he had no hesitation in reusing it over and over again.

73 Jacob's Dream, 1639
Oil on canvas, 179 x 233 cm
Museo del Prado, Madrid ,

You have to approach this picture quite closely to recognize the angelic figures in the diagonal shaft of light. They are only presented in outline, in almost the same bright color as the light. The strength of the picture is in the contrast between the earthy lower third (in color as well) and the much larger sky area with its blue, silver and yellowy-white color nuances.

NEW FEMALE TYPES

74 *Maria Aegyptiaca (St. Mary of Egypt)*, 1641
Oil on canvas, 133 x 106 cm
Musée Fabre, Montpellier

The rocky landscape in the background, which is only broken by a small piece of sky top left, emphasizes equally the isolation and spiritual inspiration of the saint.
It inevitably brings to mind El Greco, whose *Penitent Magdalene* (ill. 78) constituted a very successful prototype for this form of portrait, which was aimed directly at the viewer.

The subordinate social role of women in the 17th century is generally reflected in contemporary paintings. In view of this, it is interesting that we encounter two new types of female figure in both Ribera's secular and religious works: the saintly woman as hermit and the woman dueler.

The cult of St. Mary of Egypt (Maria Aegyptiaca) dates to around 400 A.D. in Palestine, but was disseminated in southern Italy and Rome around 610 A.D. Interest in the cult grew in Italy in the 9th century due to contact with the Byzantine world, so that the life of St. Mary of Egypt was included in the *Legenda Aurea* (1263–1273) by Jacobus de Voragine (1228/29–1298), the most important medieval collection of lives of the saints.

Voragine's account tells how a priest called Zosimus crosses the Jordan into the Palestine desert and finds Mary. In shame at her nakedness, she asks him for a cloak, and then at his request tells him her story. Born in Egypt, she had gone to Alexandria at the age of 12, living there for 17 years as a prostitute. She joined a group of pilgrims to Jerusalem, where an invisible force prevented her from entering the church, so she asked the Virgin Mary for forgiveness of her sins, promising to renounce the world. Supplied only with three loaves of bread, she had spent the following 47 years in the desert. At her request, Zosimus brings her communion, and soon afterwards she dies. Zosimus asks a meek lion for help in digging the grave, and buries her there.

Both before and during Ribera's day, the figure of Mary in her self-imposed exile was painted by other artists such as Jacopo Tintoretto (1518–1594). But the Spanish painter clearly took the subject especially to heart, as three surviving pictures from his own hand and two replicas demonstrate. In accordance with the standard Mediterranean iconography, the artist shows the saint as an old, careworn woman with her classic attributes of bread and a skull. In Central Europe, the depictions of Mary of Egypt often resemble those of Mary Magdalene, that is she is shown as a young penitent, and therefore often confused with her. In contrast with Tintoretto, who shows the saint as a tender figure integrated in an almost pleasant landscape, it is noticeable in all three Ribera versions how

he monumentalizes the saint by moving her right into the middle of the picture.

A full-length version of the *Maria Aegyptiaca* was part of a series of four works (ill. 75). A Ribera picture signed and dated 1641 shows the saint frontally as a three-quarter length figure (ill. 74). Whereas in this painting Ribera works with a very limited palette of shimmering golden chestnut tones, the final version of *Maria Aegyptiaca* of 1651 (ill. 81) has none of the hard chiaroscuro contrasts of the early work in the sensitively chosen color nuances and differentiated lighting.

However, the really astonishing thing about these works is the iconography, in which the saint appears as a hermit. She becomes thereby a female counterpart to St. Jerome in the desert, a type that did not previously exist in this form. The parallel with the life of St. Jerome is also found in the mention of a lion, which features in both lives.

What public did Ribera have in mind with these pictures? As we do not know whether the artist did the later two works speculatively or for a client, we have to confine ourselves to some thoughts on the first picture, which is better documented.

In 1658 the full-length version of *Maria Aegyptiaca* (ill. 75) was owned by a court official, Jerónimo de la Torre, secretary of state for Flanders under Philip IV. It belonged to a series that also included pictures of *John the Baptist* (ill. 76), *St. Bartholomew and Mary Magdalene*. De la Torre's collection also included other important works by Ribera, notably the picture of *St. Agnes in Prison* (ill. 77), now preserved in Dresden.

The series of four saints' pictures, among which the *Maria Aegyptiaca* belonged, was interpreted from a very early date as a deliberately contrasting depiction of the ages in men and women. Remarkably, St. Bartholomew is not pictured in the role of the tortured martyr this time. The only reference to his violent end is the knife he holds aloft. Even though the pictures are in very different states of preservation, we can see that the artist puts emphasis on the *Penitent Magdalene* (ill. 79). In her case, the correspondence between the figure and the landscape, for which there are precedents in the work of El Greco (ill. 78) is particularly successful. A great patch of bright sky narrows from the left to a point which thrusts into the darker parts of the picture.

75 *Maria Aegyptiaca (St. Mary of Egypt)*, 1641
Oil on canvas, 183 x 197 cm
Museo del Prado, Madrid

If, as a new interpretation claims, this picture along with
three other paintings was conceived as a group contrasting
the various ages of men and women, the other pictorial
elements have to be included in the same iconography.
Thus the tree stump could here too be a symbol for the last
phase of life, in deliberate contrast with the massively
growing tree in the depiction of *John the Baptist* (ill. 76).

76 John the Baptist, 1641
Oil on canvas, 184 x 198 cm
Museo del Prado, Madrid

This painting forms the male counterpart to the *Penitent Magdalene* (ill. 79) in the four-part series of the ages of men and women. As in the other paintings in the series, the proportions were changed in the 18th century.
A strip of canvas was added to the right of this one on which a typical Ribera tree stump was painted.
In fact, it is the massive tree in the center that is the foil for the figure of St. John and also serves as a suitable symbol of youth. The snow-capped peak in the background offers a delightful landscape motif, underlining Ribera's skills as a landscape painter.

A tree stump is placed between the rock and the female figure, its sparse but nonetheless obvious foliage somewhat relieving the desolation of the scene.

Quite clearly therefore the *Maria Aegyptiaca* (ill. 75) in the series for Jerónimo de la Torre, as a counterpart to the *Penitent Magdalene* (ill. 79), has the function of emphasizing once again the latter's special beauty. Only in the late half-length figure of 1651 (ill. 81) does Ribera apparently endeavor to produce a differentiated interpretation of the older woman.

The cult of St Mary of Egypt, which spread to the whole of Europe from southern Italy, seems to have enjoyed particular popularity in Naples. There was a church dedicated to her in the Pizzofalcone district. Following a reform of the female branch of the Augustinian order in Spain in 1603, five nuns from a convent of the saint were transferred to the Spanish viceroy's city to enforce the new stricter rule in their creed. As the district remained loyal to the king during the Masaniello uprising, the viceroy and victor in the conflict, Don Juan José de Austria, expressed willingness to co-finance a new building for the nuns, hitherto accommodated in temporary quarters. The plans for the church were drawn up by the architect Cosimo Fanzago (1591–1678). Although the foundation stone was laid in 1651 or 1661, the project was broken off and not completed until the 1710s. By that time, individual portraits of St. Mary of Egypt appear to have become unfashionable again, so that the high altar is not dedicated to her. She appears only as an accompanying figure to the Madonna, along with St. Augustine.

Ribera's last version of the subject, dated 1651 (ill. 81), may be linked with this building project, as there is a story establishing a connection between the painter, the viceroy and the picture. Don Juan José de Austria is supposed to have had a love affair with Ribera's daughter during his time in Naples. The liaison produced a child, who was then removed to a monastery in Madrid. The *Maria Aegyptiaca* was therefore thought to be a portrait of Ribera's dishonored daughter. It is now known that it was not Ribera's daughter but his niece, his brother's daughter, who became the regent's lover.

Another subject that marks Ribera's unusual handling of female subjects is the *Duel of the Women* (ill. 83). Dated 1686, the work is noticeably divided into foreground and background, with only two male figures on the edges standing between the two. In the stiff and emotionless depiction of the figures, but even

77 *St. Agnes in Prison*, 1641
Oil on canvas, 203 x 152 cm
Gemäldegalerie Alte Meister, Staatliche
Kunstsammlungen, Dresden

In this picture too Ribera succeeded in finding an
appropriate form for a tricky subject, i.e. one that
maintained *decoro*. It shows a saint who was displayed
naked in public because of her steadfastness to her beliefs
and whose hair grew rapidly and provided clothing
instead. In all probability, this figure of a girl was painted
from the same female model as the *Penitent Magdalene*
(ill. 79) in the Prado. Unlike Guido Reni, and like
Caravaggio, Ribera always preferred working from models.
On one occasion, he got into trouble because of this
practice, when it became known that his model for the
representation of an *Immaculate Conception* had
supposedly been the mistress of Don Juan José de Austria.

78 El Greco
Penitent Magdalene, c. 1580
Oil on canvas, 157 x 121 cm
Szépművészeti Múzeum, Budapest

El Greco's monumental individual figures of saints were
greeted with great interest in the 17th century. In the
course of his career, El Greco's various versions of the
penitent Magdalene show a growing tendency to cover
the female charms and suppress the sexual connotations.
This quite normal erotic element had been prominent in
Titian's treatment of the subject, for example. Unlike
Ribera, El Greco does not show us an individual but a
type, distinguishable for her typical gesture and above
all the moist eyes, which later became a feature of Guido
Reni's saintly depictions.

79 (facing page)
Penitent Magdalene, 1641
Oil on canvas, 182 x 149 cm
Museo del Prado, Madrid

This picture displays lighting and chromatic effects of
extraordinary quality, particularly in the treatment of the
saint's clothing. With youthfulness so prominent, the
usual attributes of asceticism, the skull and the scourge,
are strongly minimalized and it takes a close inspection to
find them. Only the pot of ointment, the saint's most
important symbol, is immediately noticeable thanks
to the bright reflections on the metal.

81 *Maria Aegyptiaca (St. Mary of Egypt)*, 1651
Oil on canvas, 88 x 71 cm
Museo Civico Gaetano Filangieri, Naples

The rigid upward gaze of the moist eyes conveys
something of the fanatical steadfastness of the saint that
distinguishes the version of this subject by Ribera in the
Musée Fabre in Montpellier. The clothing and position
beside a stone that acts as a table will have served to
identify the saint to the public. It cannot be accidental that
there are two replicas of this particular picture.

80 *Maria Aegyptiaca* (detail of ill. 81)

The subject of St. Mary of Egypt is often found with an
iconography similar to that of Mary Magdalene. Elements
of this shared iconography recur in Ribera as well: he gives
both a skull as attribute, and presents them with a notably
rough undergarment. On the other hand, this late version
of the subject of *Maria Aegyptiaca* goes quite a different
way in showing a mature woman, dispensing with the
usual erotic connotations such as the garment slipping
from the shoulder in the zeal of penitence.

more in the nature of the composition, echoes of a late
Roman relief have rightly been noted, especially since
the severe profile of the standing woman tends to
confirm this (ill. 84).

Although violence against women was largely taboo
in the 17th century, there were of course appropriate
pictures of female martyrs. Even the classical painter
Domenichino did not shrink from a particularly graphic
depiction of the *Murder of St. Agnes*. A number of works
dating this period also show famous historical or myth-
ical female figures such as Cleopatra, Lucretia or Sopho-
nisba inflicting violence on themselves. Only a few years
earlier, Rubens had painted a battle of the Amazons.

As in some of Ribera's other scenes of violence, the
duel also includes a person (on the left) who establishes
direct eye contact with the viewer. But as the roles of
aggressor and victim are not clearly allocated, neither
of the main figures gains the viewer's sympathy.

We do not yet have a satisfactory interpretation of
the scene. The picture has been linked with a historic
event in 1552, when two Neapolitan women dueled
for the love of a man in the presence of the viceroy. A
recent interpretation sees the fight as an allegory for the
numerous popular uprisings against the government in
Naples. Another interprets it as the victory of Minerva,
symbolizing the Neapolitan reformers, over Bellona as

82 Andrea Vaccaro
Roman gladiatrices
Oil on canvas, 175 x 199 cm
Museo del Prado, Madrid

In comparison with Ribera's *Duel of the Women* (ill. 83), this painting
by the Neapolitan painter Vaccaro carries a distinct erotic charge.
This is obtained by numerous bared female bodies and an
exaggerated sense of drama in the depiction of two other victims
and a mother-child pair. That Vaccaro intended to parody or
polemicize is not inconceivable. At the end of the 16th century, a
number of women had demanded more rights for their sex,
triggering off violent reactions from the male world.

83 *Duel of the Women*, 1636
Oil on canvas, 235 x 212 cm
Museo del Prado, Madrid

This painting by Ribera is particularly remarkable, and to date we
have no conclusive interpretation of it. Whereas the women with
their dramatic gestures are given pronounced sculptural qualities by
the intense light, the men behind the balustrade have a picturesque
Venetian quality. But compared with the bloody event, the posture
of almost all the figures is noticeably stiff and emotionless.
The movements of the female protagonists are almost frozen
in stone.

representative of the Spanish government and the local feudal lords that supported it. However, neither of these interpretations fits the bill. They assume a political stance which Ribera, who remained loyal to the Spanish viceroy, would scarcely have supported.

More relevant are the striking parallels with a picture ascribed to Vaccaro, which was in Naples until the 18th century but is now in the Prado in Madrid. Called *Roman gladiatrices* (*Roman Female Gladiators*) (ill. 82), it shows great similarities in both the composition and individual details. However, the sheer number of participants clearly gives a parodic slant to the subject matter.

An explanation for the new types of female figure appearing in Ribera's and Vaccaro's work can probably be found in women's demands for more rights which first became vocal in Italy at the end of the 16th century. We should however remember that life for women in the 17th century was not easy in a society wholly dominated by men. Treated as minors by their spouses and kept in social isolation, their job was mainly to bear children, in the course of which they mostly died young because of inadequate medical care. Nonetheless, at court and in the convents there was a degree of freedom that helped some to develop a new self-awareness. Thus Cremona-born Sofonisba Anguissola (1532–1625), for example, won the freedom to work as a painter at various Italian courts and even in Madrid. In the seclusion of the monastery, Teresa de Cepeda y Ahumada (St. Theresa of Avila, 1515–1582) developed into an accomplished poet and leading mystic who later comprehensively reformed her Order.

With his *Maria Aegyptiaca*, Ribera placed his art at the service of the Church, which with suitable examples sought to tie women into the existing system more strongly. So are women's demands for more rights being parodied in his *Duel of the Women*, as in Vaccaro's painting of the female gladiators?

We would normally look for evidence about Ribera's attitude towards women in his relationships with the women in his immediate environment. We know that his marriage to Caterina Azzolino y India, the daughter of distinguished Neapolitan painter Gian Bernardino Azzolino, had considerably facilitated his integration into the city's artistic life. Unfortunately, our limited knowledge of his personal relationships scarcely allows us to draw conclusions about his general attitude towards women. This is in fact another area that requires considerable research.

84 *Duel of the Women* (detail, ill. 83)

Mention is sometimes made of Venetian influences on Ribera's coloring from the 1630s and a growing classicizing austerity in the depiction of figures. This picture shows both in exemplary fashion. The victorious dueler is distinguished from her rival by the splendid color of her dress. Here it is not just the dominant, warm shimmering golden tone that fascinates but the harmony of the three colors. As a composition, a successful motif is the way some of the background heads are drawn into the foreground event by the billowing garment, although for the most part they appear, as usual, detached and uninvolved.

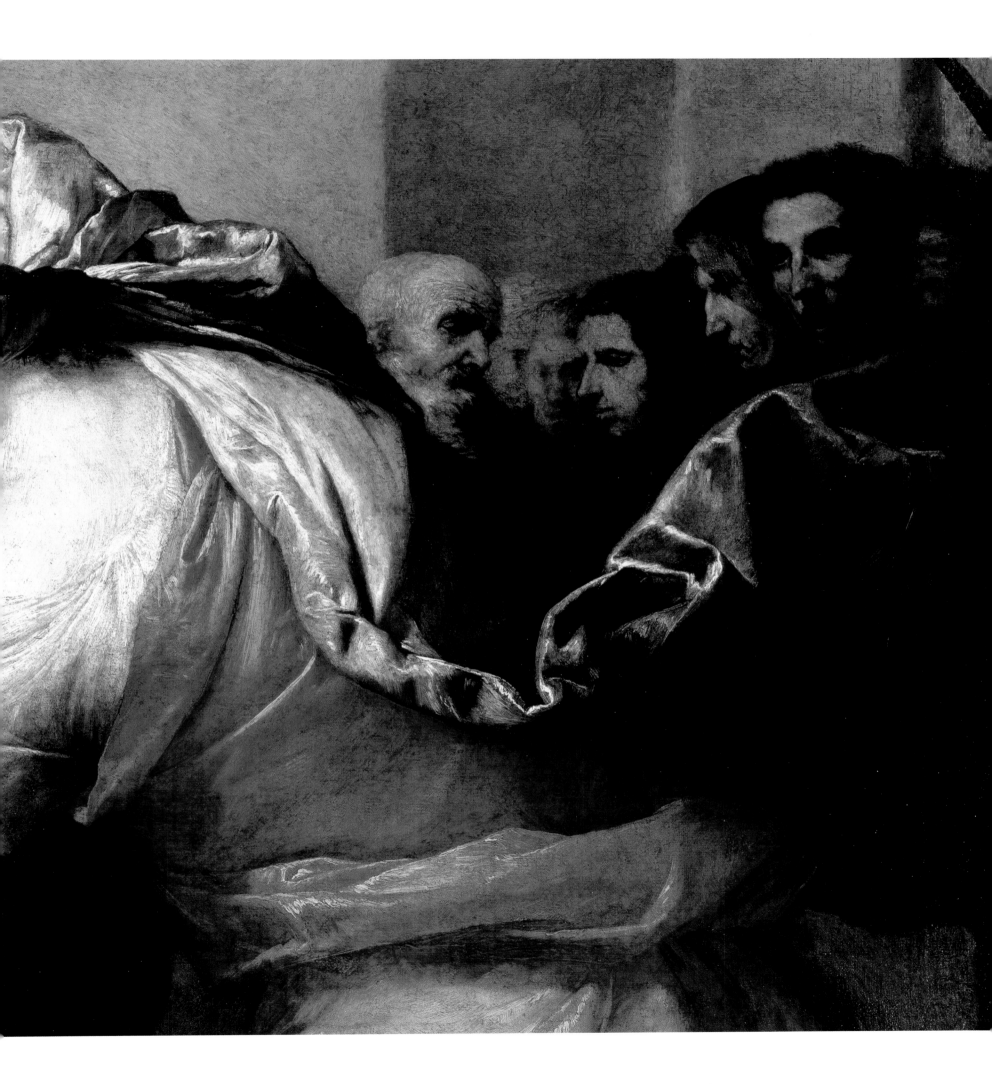

THE HISPANIC WORLD –
A COMPARISON WITH VELÁZQUEZ

85 *The Boy with the Club Foot*, 1642
Oil on canvas, 164 x 93 cm
Musée du Louvre, Paris

Despite his diminutive stature, the boy dominates the whole painting. He occupies the vertical axis so as to fill the picture, and the low horizon does the rest to monumentalize him. Three areas of the picture are particularly highlighted by the light: the deformed foot, the supplication note and the boy's smiling mouth. In this way a causal connection is suggested, namely that despite his handicap the beggar can be happy if he gets support. In this connection, the clearly unnecessary stick carries the force of a miracle, to which each viewer can contribute by way of alms.

Having looked more closely at the works of two Italian artists, Caravaggio and Reni, for their importance for Ribera's style, it would be appropriate to examine the parallels in the work of his fellow countryman Diego Velázquez in more detail. There were specific points of contact between the two in both their life and work, and indeed some surprising correspondences.

We can start from the assumption that the two artists knew each other. According to Pacheco, on his first trip to Italy in 1630 Velázquez spent some time in Naples, and must certainly have paid his famous fellow Spaniard a visit. It also seems significant that both kept in touch with the art writer Jusepe Martínez, who was friendly with Velázquez and who questioned Ribera about his art in 1625. Finally, two of the viceroys were of importance to both of them. The Duke of Alcalá was a member of the same group of learned men in Seville to which Velázquez's teacher and father-in-law Francisco Pacheco belonged, and it is possible that because of this Velázquez called on the Duke during his visit to Naples. The other viceroy, the Conde de Monterrey, received Velázquez while he was Philip IV's ambassador in Rome, and his wife, the Condesa de Monterrey, looked after the painter when he fell ill. Velázquez's portrait of her possibly dates from this time. Finally, both the Duque de Alcalá and the Conde de Monterrey may have gained support from Velázquez when they recommended that the king should buy Ribera's pictures.

In addition to these direct and indirect contacts, there are some telling biographical parallels between the two artists. Both came from relatively modest backgrounds and rose to influential positions at Spanish courts. With the succession of viceroys and the lack of a definite post at court, Ribera's was of course the more insecure position, but it left him freer to decide for himself. Furthermore, both artists spent their youth in major ports – Velázquez in Seville, Ribera in Valencia and Naples – which not only offered particularly cosmopolitan climates within the Hispanic world but were also notable for extreme social contrasts. The maritime milieu in particular offered a rich source of types and models that Ribera certainly, and the young Velázquez possibly, made use of.

How far they knew each other's work is of course difficult to assess. Velázquez must have studied Ribera's

pictorial approach very thoroughly, but Ribera was probably less familiar with the works of the ambitious younger man. It was not just during his visit to Naples that Velázquez had opportunities to study Ribera's works in the original. With the latter's growing fame, more and more of his works appeared both at court and in various Spanish collections and churches – perhaps even thanks to Velázquez's mediation. In Naples, Ribera probably only saw Velázquez's portrait of Philip IV's sister, which was painted there.

With regard to the works of the two men, many writers have commented that there are hardly any technical likenesses. Ribera's style is notable for its obsessive naturalism, which in Flemish fashion puts great emphasis on details, whereas Velázquez's brushwork is much freer and synthetic, and thus closer to Venetian painters, above all Titian.

However, in iconographical terms there are numerous parallels, though these also occur among Italian masters of the time. There are three groups of works where comparisons are informative: Ribera's beggar philosophers, his portraits of the disadvantaged and his interpretations of mythological themes using a naturalistic approach.

In the case of the beggar philosophers, the parallels are more than obvious if we compare them with Velázquez's *Menippus* (c. 1636–1640) or with his *Aesop* (c. 1636–1640). Ribera's contribution to the group of marginalized subjects includes the *Boy with the Club Foot* (ill. 85), the *Dwarf with the Dog* (ill. 86) and the *Blind Beggar and His Boy* (ill. 89). These are works depicting subjects marginalized not just by their poverty but also because of physical disability. In this respect they are comparable with most of Velázquez's "court people," a term referring to his depictions of court jesters and dwarfs.

In Ribera's *Boy with the Club Foot* (ill. 85), the subject is a young beggar, unambiguously indicated by the Latin inscription on the painted note: "Give me alms, for the love of God." To appreciate what this beggar has in common with Velázquez's "court people," it is useful to recall its differences from other contemporary depictions of the subject. Beggars were not a new subject. They occur – admittedly as negative figures – in Dutch art, particularly Dutch graphic

work. Ribera shows the young beggar and his affliction in a wholly novel way. He presents him as a full-length figure – normally the preserve of high-ranking persons – and by showing him as a happy child in a cheerful landscape, he ennobles the beggar as a thoroughly positive figure. We find a similar, if not so radical, treatment in Velázquez's portraits of court people.

Yet the decisive feature is that both artists link two different threads of artistic development, namely Dutch genre painting and the strongly moralizing religious art which predominated in southern Mediterranean countries. There are of course examples in Italian art that show that Ribera was not alone in his inversion of the Dutch beggar theme, but they are far less lavish in their execution and use of pictorial resources. For example, Francesco Villamena depicted a positive figure of a beggar, but only in a graphic work. The sum to be earned by any commission to paint a beggar was very low at the time. The general opinion was that this sort of painting required neither lavish resources nor skill. One explanation of Ribera's daring interpretation and his monumentalization of a crippled beggar boy lies in the confessional propaganda contained in his picture. In the view of the Catholic Church, the picture suggested that the viewer could win the love of God by charitable works.

Velázquez's pictures of court people are only comparable with the *Boy with a Club Foot* to a limited extent, as they belong to a genre that was not the exclusive preserve of the Seville painter. In recent years there has been a whole series of informative publications on the practice of integrating the conspicuously disabled into court life, which lasted well into the 18th century. What Velázquez's pictures do have in common with Ribera's is that they are portraits of real people, and are given special status by the choice of full-length poses. Like his colleague from Játiva, Velázquez restricted himself to a handful of attributes to identify his figures. The major emphasis was on human characterization, which reveals much understanding and sympathy, and also respect for the subject's status as an outsider.

It is more difficult to contrast the mythological works of the two artists because most of Ribera's work in this field is either lost or severely damaged. We can therefore compare four works by Velázquez: *Apollo in Vulcan's Forge, Mars, Hilanderas*, and *Triumph of Bacchus*, with only one of Ribera's, namely *Drunken Silenus* (ill. 87). The latter occupies a key position in Ribera's work because Ribera did an etching of it and sought to sell it. Art historian Enriqueta Harris has made a detailed comparative study of Ribera's *Drunken Silenus* with Velázquez's *Triumph of Bacchus* (ill. 88). The most noticeable common feature is the composition, with figures brought close to the viewer and fitted into a large format, wider than it is tall. In both cases, the main figure is the god, placed in the center of the picture with the others arranged around him. The location in both cases is a landscape: in the first, Silenus lies in front of a wine barrel, in the second Bacchus sits on one. The differences result from the divergent way the classical subject matter is linked with a naturalistic

environment. In Velázquez the classical borrowings are limited to the person of the god and perhaps the associated half-reclining figure assigned to him. Even these two figures do not correspond either in physical stature, facial type or posture to ancient conventions. Ribera, on the other hand, presents a scene such as might have been found on a Hellenistic relief, and which was enriched only with a few details and, of course, coloring. Indeed, specific antique or classical sources have been identified for Ribera: apart from a lost fresco by Giulio Romano, they include various antique sculptures. In Naples, Ribera was undoubtedly in much greater contact with the relics of antiquity than Velázquez, but the latter's links with Spanish humanists in Seville must have given him a taste for Roman antiquity as well. Both Spanish artists clearly interpret classical subjects in a naturalistic fashion so as to lend the original meaning a contemporary ironic refraction. No Italian examples of this attitude can be cited, though there are Dutch ones, if only in graphic work.

As has already been mentioned in the chapter on the *Allegory of the Five Senses*, recent research suggests that these pictures by Ribera were a source for Velázquez's *bodegones*. The question then arises whether there is any direct reference to Ribera in Velázquez's later work or whether it is in fact a case of parallel development based on a common foundation. Ribera's influencing Velázquez and vice versa are both conceivable. Ribera's *Drunken Silenus* can be dated to 1626 on the strength of the signature. His etching based on the drawing was done two years later, whereas Velázquez was working on his *Triumph of Bacchus* in 1628/29. The other pictures we have discussed were painted after the two artists met in Naples in 1630, thereby leaving much room for speculation as to how an artistic interchange may have taken place.

The suggestion of a common foundation rests on the fact that all three groups of works by Ribera and Velázquez discussed here have a common reference point in literature, principally the *Exemplary Novels* (1613) by Miguel de Cervantes (1547–1616) and the picaresque novels so popular in Spain. Carl Justi drew attention to this connection back in 1888, in his standard work *Velázquez and His Century*.

Picaresque novels are first-person narratives in which a protagonist of humble origins reviews the events of his life. Searching for a profitable occupation, he becomes familiar with other social spheres and passes critical comment on them. At the same time, both his criminal, absurd behavior and a dubious happy ending keep the reader from identifying with him, thus enabling members of the upper classes to find the text entertaining and a good read.

In the *Exemplary Novels* by Cervantes and the numerous picaresque novels, starting with *Lazarillo de Tormes* published anonymously in 1554, we meet the same sort of people as appear in Velázquez's and Ribera's pictures. We also encounter a similar ironic treatment of classical tradition, plus an attempt to bring a historical heritage up to date for contemporary readers. In both the novels and the pictures, the protagonists are

86 *The Dwarf with the Dog*, 1643
Oil on canvas, 150 x 80 cm
Former Lederer Collection, Vienna (lost)

The composition of this picture, which the art critic August L. Mayer saw in the original in Vienna and unhesitatingly ascribed to Ribera, is known to us today only from a photograph. Nonetheless, the work is of preeminent importance, since it follows similar design principles to the *Boy with the Club Foot* (ill. 85).
The subject also recalls the series of portraits of court fools and dwarfs by Velázquez, with whom Ribera clearly shared an interest in certain subjects, although technically their approaches were quite different.

87 *Drunken Silenus*, 1626
Oil on canvas, 185 x 229 cm
Museo di Capodimonte, Naples

Silenus, the corpulent, pleasure-seeking son of the Greek
god Pan, was among the constant companions of his
foster-son Dionysius (also called Bacchus). Despite his
dissipated lifestyle, a certain worldly wisdom was also
often ascribed to him. Ribera sets this mythological figure
in a complex composition filled with symbols and figures.
It has been interpreted in many different ways, none of
which satisfactorily accounts for all the elements featured.
It can definitely be said that, apart from Silenus, his father
Pan is shown in the usual iconography of half man, half
billy goat.

88 Diego Velázquez
Triumph of Bacchus, c. 1628
Oil on canvas, 165 x 225 cm
Museo del Prado, Madrid

Ribera's *Drunken Silenus* (ill. 87) is often compared with
Velázquez's *Triumph of Bacchus* because both pictures
contain a mythological theme treated so naturalistically
that a contemporary ironic allusion can be envisaged along
with the original meaning. Though there are no Italian
precedents for this, Dutch examples do exist. More
interesting are the differences between the two Spaniards.
In his *Drunken Silenus*, as in the *Arrival of Bacchus*, Ribera
quite clearly followed classical examples more closely than
Velázquez. This seems natural in that Ribera would have
encountered the artifacts of antiquity far more frequently
in Italy than Velázquez did in Spain.

simple characters who live their lives on the edge of the social abyss but cope with it with astonishing wisdom, characters whom authors and painters alike treat with obvious respect.

As *Lazarillo* was still highly popular in the 17th century, it is scarcely conceivable that Ribera should not have thought of it when he was painting his picture of the *Blind Beggar and his Boy* (ill. 89) around 1632, even if the work contains no direct references to the literary source over and above the figures. Instead, as with the *Boy with a Club Foot* (ill. 85) we find a scrap of paper that exhorts greater charity. The inscription *dies iræ, dies illa* is a quote from the words of the requiem invoking the Day of Judgment; it might therefore be seen as an unmistakable invitation to save one's soul by giving to charity. It is of course no accident that the beggar theme aroused so much attention in Italy and Spain. Once again the explanation lies in "confessionalization". Everywhere in Europe countries were busy reforming their poor laws. But whereas the Lutherans and the Calvinists (in particular) looked on poverty as largely a self-inflicted condition, the continuing advocacy of the ideal of Christian poverty in the Catholic world had a far more positive view of alms-giving and its beneficiaries. In the hope of heavenly reward, the wealthy were ready to give considerable sums to their fellow citizens in distress.

Successful examples of private and ecclesiastical charitable initiatives include the association of Pio Monte de la Misericordia, founded in 1602 in Naples, and the Hospital de la Caridad in Seville, established in the second half of the 17th century and financed by Miguel de Mañara. For the former, Caravaggio painted the central picture of the *Seven Works of Mercy* in 1607, while the artistic work for the Hospital de la Caridad was in the hands of Murillo and Juan de Valdés Leal (1622–1690). Even though Ribera did not have a comparable patron, his beggar depictions were nonetheless created in this context of improved social commitment. We must give due credit to his achievement in giving the poor an individual face. This went much beyond the hitherto wholly allegorical representations, like Caravaggio's picture. In fact, its only real comparison can be found in the new images in the literature of the time.

The comparison with contemporary Spanish literature is further supported by the fact that literature was far more highly regarded than painting in Spain. When in its chronic thirst for funds the Spanish state wanted to impose taxes on artists because of their supposed artisan status, it was the literati whose testimony saved them from the grasp of the treasury. They testified that painters worked solely for pleasure and not for Mammon. At the Madrid court, Velázquez was in direct contact with the most celebrated literary figures of the *Siglo de Oro*. A literary source of inspiration can be demonstrated for several of his pictures, and in the *Portrait of Luis de Góngora y Argote* (1561–1627) he also painted one of its most prominent representatives. Even though literary society in Naples was not as illustrious as Spain's, we may recall that Francisco de

Quevedo (1580–1645), author of the *Historia de la vida del buscón*, a picaresque novel quite as well-known as the *Lazarillo*, was employed for a while as adviser to the Duke of Osuna. As we know, the duke was Ribera's first important patron during his time in Naples from 1616–1620.

Ribera is an artist from the Hispanic world, and he shares certain ideas with some of its most prominent representatives in literature and art. But the longer he remained in Naples, the better he became at accommodating himself to his Italian colleagues.

89 *Blind Beggar and his Boy*, c. 1632
Oil on canvas, 124.5 x 101.7 cm
Allen Memorial Art Museum, Oberlin College, Oberlin/Ohio

As in the *Boy with the Club Foot*, the subject of this picture is the plea for alms. Of interest here is that there is a famous literary equivalent for the figure of the blind beggar and his boy in the picaresque novel *Lazarillo de Tormes*, published anonymously. What could be more reasonable than to trace back the many iconographical parallels between Ribera and Velázquez to their common shaping by Spanish literature? It is a characteristic feature of the art of the Hispanic world, unlike that of Italy, that not only did it derive important inspiration from literature but artists found their most persuasive spokesmen in the writers of the *Siglo de Oro*.

90 Michele Regolia
The Interior of a Palace
Oil on canvas
Private collection, Naples

Today we can scarcely conjure up a comprehensive picture of the wealth of paintings found in Naples in the 17th century. Too many works left the city in later times. Unfortunately there also scarcely any pictures that, like Dutch pictures of the time, might convey an impression of how the works of art were presented in private galleries. As with reconstructions of what subjects formed the principal content, we have to rely on assessments of the numerous written sources.

Art collections in southern Italy have recently been the subject of a very informative investigation by Gérard Labrot. A comparison of the contents of the galleries up to the mid-17th century with those of Roman collectors showed a markedly lower proportion of pictures with mythological themes and, conversely, more pictures with religious content (ill. 90). Similar results from corresponding investigations for the Iberian peninsula prove that the parallel is no mere accident. The similarities of content and theme in the various collections demonstrate the structural similarity of patronage and social environment in both parts of the Hispanic world.

The structural similarity lies in the fact that a culture of art collecting based on expert knowledge existed neither in Madrid nor Naples at the time in question, even though, in Madrid at least, the demand for pictures was enormous. In both places there were only a few outstanding patrons, but they had huge funds at their disposal and by their choice steered others in a particular direction. In the Iberian Peninsula, they were mainly the ruling Habsburgs, in southern Italy the current viceroys, a few ecclesiastical institutions and especially the Antwerp-born merchant Gaspar Roomer, the richest man in Naples, who at the time of his death owned about 1,500 pictures.

The comparable social environments included the powerful presence of ecclesiastical institutions in public life. They quite consciously used pictures to convey the tenets of Catholic faith, but over and above this developed

a certain inquisitorial mentality of self-censorship that rendered controls virtually unnecessary. This quite clearly also had an influence on the preferences of collectors. Thus they not only preferred religious themes but also eschewed provocative depictions.

A central point of clerical criticism since the Council of Trent concerned nudes. In the religious sphere, it was practically impossible to paint them, because of the requirements of maintaining *decoro* and keeping secular and religious subjects distinct. But even in the secular sphere, attempts were made to put subtle pressure on collectors. These campaigns reached a peak in 1632 with the publication in Madrid of a survey among university teachers concerning the pros and cons of nudes. The intention was to bring moral authority to bear on the aristocracy, otherwise out of reach, and prick their consciences. By this date commissions for mythological pictures were already markedly in decline, but now even existing works gradually disappeared from the collections.

However, the strict attitude towards nudes should not mislead us into thinking that all religious art had to follow established norms, rather in the manner of an index of proscribed pictures. Although the Catholic world avoided open quarrels between secular authority and ecclesiastical representatives, widely differing positions could be adopted under one and the same papal roof. This especially concerned religious questions and therefore their representation as well, as transpired in the dispute over the

91 Giovanni Lanfranco
Dome fresco, 1643
Cappella del Tesoro di San Gennaro, Naples Cathedral

The choice of the artists was intended to underline the importance of the project when the Cappella di San Gennaro was decorated. The prevailing low opinion of the local Neapolitan School and prominent reputation of the nearby Roman lobby made the choice easy. It was only after the mysterious death of Domenchino, the big name brought in from the papal city, that local painters such as Ribera got a look in.

92 Salvator Rosa (1615-1673)
Seascape
Oil on canvas, 44 x 62 cm
Museo Nazionale di San Martino, Naples

Salvator Rosa, who trained in Ribera's workshop and later
worked as a painter, writer and musician, was one of the
most important figures in Italian painting in the 17th
century. Although he later left Naples, it was there that he
acquired his preference for a naturalistic style. In pictures
such as this coastal landscape, the influence of Ribera's
style and paintings in Gaspar Roomer's collection can be
discerned. Roomer, whose collection acted as a cultural
interchange, brought new pictorial subject matter such as
seascapes with him from his homeland in the Netherlands.

doctrine of the *Immaculate Conception* which was so
important for Ribera's paintings.

Two further aspects of art collecting were typical of the
situation in Naples: first, the unequal contest with Rome
which caused the prolonged neglect of local artists, and
secondly the conspicuous presence of a neo-Caravag-
gesque naturalistic style.

The late development of a distinct Neapolitan school in
the mid-17th century was principally due to a shortage of
patrons willing to provide consistent support to regional
artists and influence the style of their output. This lack of
interest in the home market can be attributed to the high
reputation of Roman art, which initially wholly dominated
nearby Naples. A similar situation prevailed in Spain,
though there it was not the proximity of Rome but the
legend of it that hampered the discovery of native talents.
Virtually all the monastic orders in Naples had close
connections with the Vatican, and were therefore tuned to
Vatican aesthetic tastes (ill. 91). The same applied to the
Spanish viceroys, who generally reached Naples via the
ambassadorial post to the papal court. If even local
patrons showed little desire to purchase local work, preferring that of Roman painters, how could collectors who
were initially outsiders find their way to local art?

Allusion has already been made to the rapid development of art in Rome as a result of the successive popes'
relatively short terms in office, which constantly brought
new groups to power and therefore favored a high degree
of rivalry between the artists in favor at any time. However,
seductive as the parallel seems, the situation cannot be
compared with the frequent changes of government in
Naples. Unlike the new popes, the viceroys had no
standing patronage system to tap into, where art had its
acknowledged place in the process of mutual promotion.
They came to the city only to take up office, and were in
power too briefly to establish long-term artistic patronage.

Ultimately, there are various reasons why the influence
of naturalism proved so durable in Naples. Initially, the
impression of Caravaggio's work must have lasted longer
than in Rome, simply because no school of painting had
hitherto existed with its own aesthetic categories. In addition, the foundations laid by Caravaggio were quickly built
on and developed by a major painter, namely Jusepe de
Ribera, who himself acquired numerous imitators among
regional artists.

And finally, the particular artistic inclination of the
patrons was important, because they were in a position of
monopoly and power. The Spanish viceroys were already
familiar with strikingly reality-oriented paintings from their
homeland, whose enduring impression was refined by the
experiences of Rome but never wholly extinguished. This
applies to the Duque of Alcalá as well, whom we must
thank for the development of a naturalistic "theory of art"
by Ribera.

The influence of Gaspar Roomer for his part was
twofold. Not only did he support regional artists, but he
also offered them the chance to study in his gallery. His art
collection in Naples must have served the same function as
the royal collection in Madrid. But whereas Spanish artists
mainly had the chance to see works imported from Italy in
the rich collections in the royal palaces, Roomer offered an
acquaintance with the art of northern Europe.

As a Netherlander, Roomer acquired the naturalistic perspective in his cradle, and the scenes of violence also seem, in the opinion of art historian Francis Haskell, to have found a special champion in him. He did occasionally buy pictures in Rome, of course, but the classical and neo-Venetian schools prevailing there did not especially interest him. Instead, one of his greatest merits was to familiarize local artists more closely with the classic painting genres of the north (such as seascapes, battle scenes, landscapes (ill. 92), hunting pieces and still lifes) and to introduce them to the works of Rubens and van Dyck as well.

Only after Ribera's death, i.e. in the second half of the 17th century, did the art collections of southern Italy and the Iberian Peninsula develop in different directions, while the positions of Naples and Rome drew appreciably closer once again. Whereas religious themes continued to predominate in Madrid, landscape, still life (ill. 93) and genre painting became more important. In addition, mythological and religious paintings now often hung side by side in the same rooms, which indicates the primacy of aesthetic rather than religious preoccupations.

93 Giovanni Battista Recco
Still life with the head of a billy goat, c. 1650
Oil on canvas, 128 x 180 cm
Museo di Capodimonte, Naples

The work of Recco, a painter of whose life we know nothing, is basically known only in two paintings, signed and dated by him 1653 and 1654. His still lifes with simple everyday objects were possibly prompted by similar Spanish work, e.g. of Francisco Zurbarán. How such influence might have been transmitted has yet to be clarified. After Ribera's death there was growing interest in Naples in secular subjects, and Recco may have profited from this.

CULTURAL INTERACTION WITH ITALIAN ARTISTS IN NAPLES AND SALAMANCA

94 *Earthly Trinity*, c. 1626
Oil on canvas, 393 x 262 cm
Appartamento Storico del Palazzo Reale, Naples

The history of this picture has only recently been reconstructed. Ribera painted it for the convent of Trinità delle Monache in Naples. The title refers to a representation of Mary, Joseph, and the Christ Child as an entity corresponding to the heavenly trinity of God the Father, Son, and Holy Spirit. Indeed, there is a further work by the artist with a bust-length God the Father that was intended as a counterpart to the present picture but was probably painted later. The picture was painted for a marble retable by Cosimo Fanzago, and constitutes the first collaboration by two artists whose work was later so closely linked.

From a present-day perspective, our preoccupation with footloose painters such as El Greco and Rubens can easily mislead us into thinking that artists in the 16th and 17th centuries were mobile and flexible in a very modern way. We forget that it was never easy for an artist at that time to establish himself in a strange city. For example, entrenched local artists demanded that Zurbarán, who came from Extremadura, subject himself to an examination by local painters when he wanted to work in Seville, even though by then he had proven his proficiency several times over. Domenichino had an even harder time of it when he was summoned to Naples to work on the Real Cappella del Tesoro di San Gennaro. After he had taken up the invitation against the bitter opposition of local artists, he received repeated murder threats, and indeed died without completing his work, under circumstances that were never fully explained. Ribera himself was accused of having murdered him.

How then could a painter from Játiva establish himself in Naples and even rise to become one of the city's most distinguished painters? Ribera always remained an outsider in the local art world. During his first years in Naples, he did not receive a single commission from the city institutions, nor from the well-endowed churches and monasteries where most Naples-based artists found work. Instead, his most important patrons, like the viceroys, came from other corners of the Hispanic world or territories politically close to it.

That he was nonetheless able to achieve some degree of integration appears to have been due to two important contacts: his personal connection with the respected artist Gian Bernardino Azzolino through his marriage, and the artistic co-operation with the sculptor and architect Cosimo Fanzago, who came from Bergamo, not Naples.

Ribera's co-operation with Fanzago probably began in the late 1620s, when both were working on the interior of the church of Trinità delle Monache in Naples. At the time, Ribera was painting his *Earthly Trinity* (ill. 94) for the sculptor's marble retable, but the two most important joint projects actually date from the first half of the 1630s, when Ribera had moved on to a brighter, more light-imbued style. In 1635, the painter delivered five pictures for the ornamentation of the Conde de Monterrey's burial chapel in Salamanca, which was built to a design by Fanzago. From 1637, Ribera was involved in the work on the Certosa di San Martino in Naples, for which Fanzago did the sculptural work. Nicola Spinosa has endeavored to show that the two artists not only worked alongside each other several times but also adopted similar formal features in their work. An example of this is the idealized portrait of St. Bruno, which Ribera painted twice in a very similar fashion, once in the *Earthly Trinity* and the other some time years earlier, in 1624, in the *Madonna with the Christ Child and St. Bruno* (ill. 95). Fanzago's counterpart was a monumental bust of the saint for the Certosa in San Martino (ill. 96).

In Salamanca, Fanzago acted both as architect and sculptor. He and a colleague designed the whole church and monastic site of the Agustinas Recoletas where the burial chapel for the viceroy was to be. The job included the main retable for the church, with its crucifixion group (ill. 98). Installed in the central axis of the retable were two paintings by Ribera: the large *Immaculate Conception* in the center (ill. 62) and a *Pietá* above it. For the same project, Ribera also did his *St. Januarius in Glory* (ill. 66), plus pictures of *St. Augustine* for a side altar and a further *Immaculate Conception* for the monastic building.

The first steps in the planning were prompted by the eruption of Vesuvius in December 1631, an event that not only made the Count of Monterrey aware of his mortality but also awoke a feeling of gratitude to St. Januarius, who was generally credited with sparing Naples (ill. 105). Probably the viceroy only initially intended a retable for his family church in Salamanca, but as work was proceeding in 1635 his vision expanded into a larger project.

Ribera succeeded in completing his part by 1637, though building work continued into the early 18th century. Neither Fanzago nor Ribera themselves went to Salamanca. On-site direction was handled by an architect imported from Italy who worked on behalf of Fanzago. Even so, the project must have brought the two artists in Naples closer together, and naturally helped to familiarise their work in Spain.

Widely differing sources have been cited as the model for Ribera's *Immaculate Conception* (ill. 62). The picture by Rubens painted in Madrid and suggested by Suzanne Stratton has only the dynamic movement of the drapery in common with Ribera's work. Ribera scholar Craig Felton proposes the version painted in Rome by Guido Reni in 1627 for the Duke of Alcalá, later the viceroy of Naples, but this shows few compositional correspondences.

The most noticeable parallel to Ribera's composition, the use of two diagonally rising angels, is found in a picture by Giovanni Lanfranco (1582–1647), which Pérez Sánchez, probably correctly, cites as a convincing direct model. The picture was painted between 1628 and 1630 for the Roman church of the Capuchins, but was destroyed by fire in 1813, which probably explains why it has not previously featured in the discussion. Its design is known through a copy, various graphic works, the preparatory drawings and two surviving fragments (ill. 97). A native of Parma, Lanfranco settled in Naples in 1634 and worked together with Ribera on several projects. He also painted an *Annunciation* for the same viceroy, the Conde de Monterrey, who commissioned the *Immaculate Conception* from Ribera.

In the case of the Certosa di San Martino, the work was a reconstruction of an existing monastery. Fanzago was occupied on the job from 1623 to 1656, though the first plans dated back to 1618. An even harder task than in Salamanca, it fell to the sculptor to combine the very heterogeneous artistic contributions into a single program of works, which basically consisted of two parts: cladding the whole interior with polychrome marble panels (ill. 101), and producing and installing a series of statues, which included the *St. Bruno* mentioned above (ill. 96).

In 1637 Ribera painted the *Pietá* (ill. 99), which was hung above the altar of the sacristy richly ornamented by Fanzago. In 1638 there followed the commission for the series of 14 prophets and patriarchs in the interior of the church, which were completed by 1643. Because of his grave illness, the artist was only able to complete other pictures ordered at the same time, the *Communion of the Apostles* (ill. 100) plus pictures of *St. Jerome* and *St. Sebastian*, in 1651, shortly before his death.

The outstanding position of Ribera's works in the Certosa reflects his status in Naples. He must have seen the opportunity to place numerous works of his own alongside Neapolitan and outside artists as a special challenge.

Nicola Spinosa rightly draws attention to the same forceful energy in the series of prophets and patriarchs (ills. 102, 103) as is evident in the cycles of philosophers and apostles from around 1630 (ills. 63, 64). At the same time, however, he also discerns in these later pictures by the mature artist a more intense distillation of universal human experiences than in his earlier works. This claim is only suspect inasmuch as the prophets and patriarchs, like Fanzago's saints, are far more distanced from the viewer than the beggar philosophers. The distancing is the effect of their profound absorption in study and also the monumental design. Whereas the beggar philosophers carry the marks of tough living in their persons and their clothing and command respect for being based in real life, the figures in the Certosa di San Martino appear in a trance. Their expression follows an old, familiar traditional iconography of philosophers, whose depiction deploys mighty beards and numerous books and scrolls to convince the public of the subjects' importance. Figures such as *Joel and Amos* (ills. 102, 103) in the Certosa exact attention for their artistic design or even admiration for their achievement, but they do not carry the fascinating conviction that distinguishes Ribera's early works.

The change from "true" to "well-executed" pictures suggested by a comparison of this sort may be seen entirely as the result of the changed circumstances of Ribera the social climber. By the late 1630s, the Bohemian Ribera of the past was long gone. In 1625 he had accepted the honorary Order of Christ from the pope, and by then was far removed from his Spanish roots as a cobbler's son – although in 1638, for reasons unknown, he allowed his origins to be explicitly confirmed by the Inquisition. He had by then become one of those artists who enjoyed much greater esteem in Italy than in Spain, where painters were still often equated with artisans and paid accordingly.

Ribera succeeded in becoming integrated in Naples, at least for a time, because his arrival in 1616 allowed him to benefit from the important artistic legacy of Caravaggio. If we accept Spinosa's hypothesis, it is largely due to Ribera that new life was breathed into naturalism in the city just when it appeared to be losing momentum. The artist was clearly aware of the difference between his individual style and the Roman classical style, and like his origins turned it to advantage. Initially he may have been fascinated by Caravaggio's style, but from 1632 he used it as only one of several stylistic options. In his later years, for example, he did not hesitate to continue using Caravaggio's tenebrism whenever the subject matter required it. Conversely, he was also ready to make concessions to the client's taste as circumstances demanded. This ability to adapt was particularly evident in his work for the Real Capella del Tesoro.

When Domenichino took over the commission, all the earlier works had been removed so that a homogeneous interior could be created. When Domenichino died suddenly in 1641, it was essential to maintain continuity. Ribera and Stanzione were initially commissioned to report on the state of the works. Subsequently they were each commissioned to paint a large picture for the side altars on silver-plated copper supports. At their recommendation the most important job, the redesign of the ceiling painting, was given to Lanfranco. Ribera's picture *St. Januarius Emerges Unharmed from the Fiery Furnace* (ills. 105, 106) is probably the most classical work he ever did.

The work represents a compromise by Ribera, but it was by no means a betrayal of his principles. Despite critical comments in the literature, he did not adapt his

96 Cosimo Fanzago
St. Bruno, c. 1631
Marble
Certosa di San Martino, Naples

This bust was designed for the Certosa, the Carthusian monastery in Naples. It is part of a series of five pictures of Carthusian saints there, who were installed over various doorways. Nicola Spinosa compares this idealized portrait with two portraits of the saint in works by Ribera, the *Earthly Trinity* and the *Madonna with the Christ Child and St. Bruno*, to show that both artists had similar objectives in their formal language.

95 (facing page)
The Madonna with the Christ Child and St. Bruno, 1624
Oil on canvas, 205 x 153.5 cm
Schlossmuseum, Kunstsammlung zu Weimar, Weimar

This picture is not only signed but dated, though the date was long read as 1634 rather than 1624. In support of the earlier date is the great similarity between the kneeling saint worshipping the Christ Child and the figure of St. Bruno in the *Earthly Trinity* (ill. 94). The similar physiognomies of the two figures suggests that Ribera used the same person as a model here.

97 Giovanni Lanfranco
Immaculate Conception, 1628-1630
Pen, brown wash, white highlights, 56 x 41 cm
Museum der bildenden Künste, Leipzig

It is principally the dynamism of representation in the
billowing garments and the angels facing this way and that
which links Lanfranco's *Immaculate Conception* with
Ribera's treatment of the subject (ill. 62). It is at the same
time quite distinct from the earlier rather static tradition
of representation found typically in the versions of the
Seville painter Francisco Pacheco or even his pupil and
son-in-law Diego Velázquez.

98 Cosimo Fanzago, Jusepe de Ribera et al.
Main retable (overall view), c. 1635
Church of the Convento de las Agustinas Recoletas de
Monterrey, Salamanca

The project was in fact a close collaboration between
Ribera and Fanzago in Naples, the latter acting both as
architect and sculptor. He designed the main retable for
the church. It is surmounted by a crucifixion group, above
two pictures by Ribera: in the center is the great painting
of the *Immaculate Conception* (ill. 62), and above it a *Pietà*.
The other four paintings in the high altar were likewise
commissioned from Neapolitan artists.

99 (facing page)
Pietà, 1637
Oil on canvas, 264 x 170 cm
Certosa di San Martino, Naples

The decoration of the Certosa di San Martino was one of the most
prestigious projects for Neapolitan artists in the 1630s. In 1637
Ribera was commissioned to do the *Pietà*, which was hung over the
altar of the sacristy, newly (and richly) refurbished by Fanzago.
The artist had to compete for the job when the work for the
monastery was commissioned.

100 *Communion of the Apostles*, 1651
Oil on canvas, 400 x 400 cm
Certosa di San Martino, Naples

The commission for the *Communion of the Apostles* was, like that for
the prophets and patriarchs, given to Ribera at the end of the 1630s,
but because of a grave illness he was only able to complete it shortly
before his death. The work shows a marked classicizing tendency.

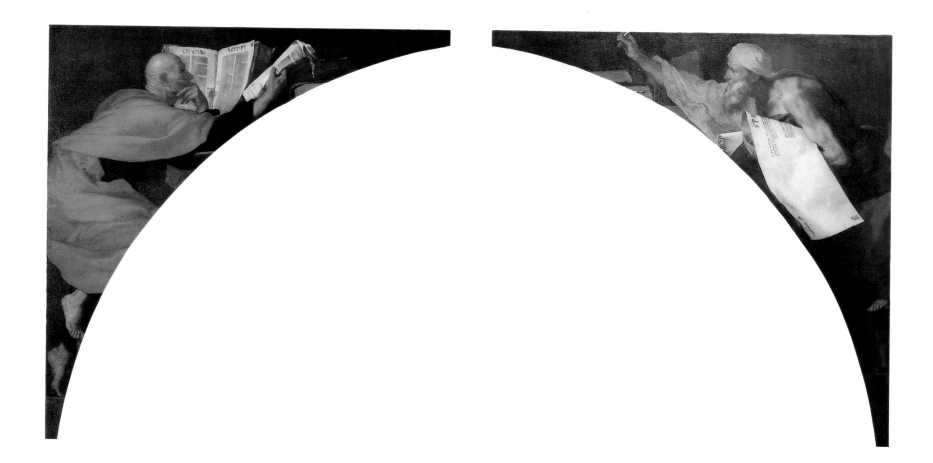

technique to Domenchino manner, which he vehemently rejected, but to Lanfranco's, whose ceiling paintings set the style for the whole chapel. It is evident that Fanzago and Lanfranco, the artists with whom he carried out several joint projects, were Ribera's main artistic points of reference in Naples. In his second, post-1632 period, they became real collaborators in place of Ribera's "virtual" partners Caravaggio and Velázquez.

In conclusion, we can safely say that while he was in Naples, Ribera remained a foreigner who knew how to fit in. He therefore no doubt acted correctly in taking refuge in the viceroy's palace during the Masaniello uprising. His clients were only to a very small extent the same as those of local artists. Even the *Allegory of the Five Senses* (ill. 2, 20, 21 and 23) was sold to a Spaniard, and later it was again people from the Hispanic world rather than southern Italians who showed interest in his work. Ribera became friendly with Italian artists, but the most important of them, Cosimo Fanzago and Giovanni Lanfranco, were not from Naples either. It is therefore no accident that we continue to find his brother Juan Ribera and for a while the Valencian Juan Do and the Fleming Enrico Semmer in his workshop.

Ribera probably picked up the basis of his naturalistic style during his time in Valencia and northern Italy, with the result that in Rome he mingled with Flemish artists who, like him, enthused about Caravaggio's new style. Although the pictures he painted in the 1630s clearly displayed more color and light, it was his commitment to reality that continued

to inspire him. Both the late examples of a consciously revived tenebrism and the choice of themes, the beggar philosophers and the many pictures of violence, testify to this. In these, he sought to reflect the social tensions that he had experienced in Naples and which burst into flame in the Masaniello uprising. As our analysis of the portrait of *Magdalena Ventura* (ill. 49) showed, in Ribera's case "naturalism" did not mean copying what he saw but starting from reality and interpreting it artistically "in wonderful fashion."

Among his contemporaries, it is not the works of Reni or Poussin that are most akin to his, but those of Velázquez. The correlations in these are not fortuitous but actual connections, as is shown by the influence of his *Allegories of the Five Senses* (ills. 2, 20, 21 and 23) on Velázquez's *bodegones*, such as *The Water Seller of Seville* (ill. 24). The basis for this spiritual affinity may have been the similar cultural climate of the three Hispanic ports of Seville, Valencia and Naples. The intercommunication and theoretical underpinning of artistic content were provided by Pacheco and the Duke of Alcalá, among others. Above all, a common basis was created by Spanish literature, read throughout Europe at the time, and it is therefore no wonder that the protagonists of the picaresque novel and the dispassionate irony of Cervantes are also found in the work of both artists. In many respects, Ribera made important contributions to a new iconography of Catholic visual propaganda by bringing together differing cultural traditions, such as with his depictions of the Immaculate Conception. Ribera's art historical importance and his most enduring effect on today's viewer are most

102, 103 *Joel and Amos*, 1638-1643
Oil on canvas, each 265 x 235 cm
Certosa di San Martino, Naples

It is worth comparing the idealized portraits of the prophets and patriarchs, painted on canvas to fit into the spandrels of the arches, with the pictures of the apostles and philosophers in the smaller-format paintings. Initially they appear to have a good deal in common, such as the individual designs of the heads, the well-thumbed books and manuscripts and the plain dress that nonetheless captivates the viewer by its exquisite coloration. Only then do the differences appear all the more marked: the people in the paintings are generally in much closer contact with the viewer, not only because they look directly at him, but also because they have an earthbound solidity. The figures in the Certosa are totally absorbed in their studies, and with their narrow, elongated bodies represent a wholly spiritual state.

101 (facing page)
Cosimo Fanzago and Jusepe de Ribera
Wall decoration, 1637-1652

Church interior, Certosa di San Martino, Naples
Ribera's ambitious series of paintings of prophets and patriarchs in the Certosa church have been appropriately compared with Fanzago's sculptures for the same building. In both cases we see bodies shrouded in broad robes, artfully animated, reminiscent of Michelangelo's ceiling paintings in the Sistine Chapel in Rome. They appear as much a credible expression of spiritual endeavor as protagonists in a subtle aesthetic game.

104 *St. Januarius in Glory* (detail of ill. 66)
St. Januarius, the most important patron of Naples, was popularly venerated mainly for his protection of the city during the eruptions of Vesuvius. During the Masaniello uprising, attempts were made to dampen down social eruptions as well with his assistance, by exhibiting his head relic and blood. In the painting, a putto at the saint's feet lifts up a chest with the miracle-working blood on it.

105 (facing page)
St. Januarius Emerges Unharmed from the Fiery Furnace, 1646
Oil on copper, 320 x 200 cm
Cappella del Tesoro di San Gennaro, Naples Cathedral

It was intended to refurbish the Cappella del Tesoro in a homogeneous style. Ribera therefore had to compromise, and consequently produced probably the most classical work in his career. This relates not just to the coloration and the light but also to the variety of anatomical forms and rhetorical gestures, which must have been preceded by comprehensive studies. The statuesque figure of the saint, who seems electrically charged from the flames, is contrasted dramatically with the gestures of the distraught persecutors.

clearly evident in the new type of "street philosopher." Originally developed in the context of Catholic "confessionalization," they represent a special challenge even today.

In works such as *Boy with the Club Foot* (ill. 85) he combined subjects from secular Dutch genre painting with religious art, in the service of compassion. That he found such a vivid form for this may have as much to do with his simple origins as with his independence, which he was able to preserve as a result of the constant change of client. Unlike Velázquez and others, he enjoyed the benefits of a princely court without having to pay for his social rise with numerous non-artistic services.

The role of the court patronage system has been emphasized by art historians to such an extent in recent years that court artists have enjoyed a rather unmerited and certainly indiscriminatory upgrading in comparison with their colleagues. In fact a model developed for Italian courts is applied unreliably to other countries.

The Spanish court was conservative, and anyone seeking artistic freedom in Spain was advised to steer clear of it. Although both Ribera and Velázquez ennobled the ordinary man in their early work and later painted philosophers dressed as picaros, there are also differences between them. If we look for further examples of human sympathy in their works, we soon encounter in Velázquez only court figures, whereas Ribera's eye remained on the lower classes. The example of a new iconography for the *Maria Aegyptiaca* (ill. 74), her depiction as an emaciated old woman, highlights this clearly.

Particular attention has been paid to Ribera's artistic development from his early days to the 1640s, as during this period he drew his artistic vigor from the combination of different cultural traditions and a wide range of stylistic modes. In later years he was still open to new ideas, but stylistically he relied increasingly, no doubt in part due to his established status, on his celebrated, mostly classically orientated colleagues in both Naples and Rome. A good example of this is the picture *St. Januarius Emerges Unharmed from the Fiery Furnace* (ill. 105). In his critical involvement with the Roman–Bolognan classical school, Ribera had no problem in maintaining a distinction between artistic stances that he was ready to accept, such as those of Reni and Lanfranco, and others he continued to reject, like that of Domenichino.

Ribera's development has been outlined here in terms of style and content. In stylistic terms, two successive phases can be distinguished. Initially Ribera deployed his naturalistic inclination to combine the chiaroscuro style of Caravaggio with elements of classicism, mainly in the style of Reni, though certain reservations must be made even here. From 1632, a new interpretation of light and color becomes apparent in Ribera's work, in which he was probably reacting principally to a neo-Venetian trend centered on Castiglione and his associates in Rome.

In terms of content, a chronology is incomparably more difficult, and every pictorial subject requires an attentive analysis of its own. Thus it is only at first sight that the 1637 series of *Allegories of the Five Senses* appear to be a counterpart of the series of works on the same subject from his Roman period. Even though the popular Neapolitan figure of the *Girl with the Tambourine* (ill. 108), here intended as an allegory of hearing, is depicted with great lifelikeness, she lacks the special emotional involvement and human complicity that characterized the earlier works. The earthy gaze has indeed become "folksy."

On the other hand, in the portrait of *Magdalena Ventura* (ill. 49), the *Adoration of the Shepherds* (ill. 107) dated 1640, and his late saints, such as *St. Jerome Penitent* (ill. 109), which was painted in the last year of his life, we encounter the same truth to life that commanded respect in the two versions of *Democritus* (ills. 52, 54). Like most strangers in an alien place, Jusepe de Ribera sought contact mainly with his own kind and less with the locals. First there were the many followers of Caravaggio from far and wide, then later

107 *Adoration of the Shepherds*, 1640
Oil on canvas, 226 x 317 cm
Patrimonio Nacional, Monasterio de San Lorenzo el Real
de El Escorial

This picture along with another on the same subject is
preserved in the monastery at the Escorial. For a long
time, its bad state of conservation and difficulties of
access prevented a definite attribution to Ribera. Other
supposed authors included his pupil or colleague
Juan Do. The most recent restoration now leaves
Ribera's authorship in no doubt.

106 *St. Januarius Emerges Unharmed from the Fiery
Furnace* (detail, ill. 105)

Quite clearly, and in contrast with the usual iconography,
it is not putti (top right) or other heavenly messengers that
proclaim the miracle that has just occurred but the great
patch of color of the sky itself. Significantly the head of
St. Januarius breaks into this heavenly sphere, while the
persecutors, crowded into a confined space, are literally
cast to the ground, their limbs forming a thoroughly
disjointed tangle of human limbs.

mainly Fanzago from Bergamo and Lanfranco from
Parma. His cultural achievements brought him recognition in the city and beyond. What ultimately made
him indispensable and protected him from marginal-
ization, even after the uprising against the Spanish
viceroy, was his role as a model for younger artists.

Ribera's role between cultures is perhaps most easily
compared with Rubens. Both painters were able to
exploit to their advantage the geographical breadth of
the territories ruled from Madrid. Ribera's role as an
intermediary between the Iberian Peninsula and the
Netherlands/Italy, and his success in both, entitles us to
consider him, like Rubens, a new type of "artistic
nomad" who made a vital contribution to disseminating confessional iconography in the 17th century
and who is nowadays experiencing a resurrection in the
train of globalization.

108 *Girl with the Tambourine (Allegory of Hearing)*, 1637
Oil on canvas, 59 x 45 cm
Private collection, London

As Ribera climbed the social scale, his genre pictures changed from an earthy directness to folksiness. This picture is one of the *Allegories of the Five Senses* dating from 1637, and is particularly interesting as a comparison with the earlier one of 1613. The artist is not making fun of the then popular Neapolitan figure of the girl with the tambourine, but he no longer seeks her complicity. The street children in Murillo are depicted in the same way, their hard lives prettified for artistic consumption and picturesquely ennobled. Their tatty clothing is seen as an exotic attribute, not as a challenge to ponder the purpose and meaning of life.

109 *St. Jerome Penitent*, 1652
Oil on canvas, 77 x 71 cm
Museo del Prado, Madrid

This picture was painted in the last year of Ribera's life, and there is much to suggest that he identified with the figure of the saint. Interestingly, we are shown a wholly new type of St. Jerome who is quite clearly distinct from earlier versions. He has a narrow face, thick white facial hair and an artistically arranged full beard. At the same time, the work is a last, outstanding example of the artist's individual style. In it, he harmoniously blends a revived Caravaggesque chiaroscuro with an inner brightness drawn from Flemish and Venetian painting.

DRAWINGS AND PRINTED GRAPHICS

110 *Acrobats on the Rope*, c. 1634/35
Pen with brown gouache on yellowish paper,
25.7 x 19.8 cm
Real Academia de Bellas Artes de San Fernando, Madrid

This picture is possibly a spontaneous record of an event that Ribera chanced to see in the streets of Naples. In these artistic jottings, he once again uses his typical, restless stroke of the pen that leaves the outlines of the figures open. Some parts are given a brush wash, lending the work an individual brightness.

Given this background, it comes as no surprise that Ribera's graphic work is hardly typically "Italian" either, but again the result of sundry cultural influences. That applies to both his drawings and the printed graphics. Compared with the output of the graphic work of many Roman artists, Ribera's production of the hundred or so sheets currently known is very modest. But in this Ribera is typical of the whole Neapolitan art scene, and we find the same lack of surviving drawings in Spain as well. Yet several factors indicate that he placed great importance on drawing, and that there were once far more works by him. Tending to confirm this is the fact that we have far more graphic works by his pupils Salvator Rosa and Luca Giordano, who turned their backs on Naples for a while. Moreover, the variety of the surviving drawings by Ribera and the fact that contemporaries highly esteemed his graphic work suggest the same thing.

Because of the lack of Spanish examples for comparison, it is difficult to know where to place Ribera as a graphic artist. If we accept the view of the Prado curator Manuela B. Mena Marqués, his graphic works betray traces of Flemish painting, in their obvious interest in light and reality, which had a particularly strong effect in Spain. She finds Ribera's work much closer to Italian graphic work, especially that of artists from Parma and Rome, than to the "Spanish school".

In fact, unlike Caravaggio and Velázquez, Ribera prepared his oil paintings with drawings. The drawings for the pictures of *Apollo and Marsyas* (ill. 45) and *Samson and Delilah* (ill. 111) represent different stages of this preparatory work. The latter is executed virtually as a picture in its own right, and would have served as a test piece for a potential client. That Ribera used models of this kind is known from a surviving document. The relationship between some preparatory drawings and the completed pictures, plus the fact that several of the sheets are dated, has enabled us to put Ribera's graphic oeuvre in chronological order. Mena Marqués distinguishes two phases: the first in which the artist produced carefully designed, richly detailed drawings done mostly in red chalk and black pencil; and a second phase from the late 1620s when the artist more often used pen and brush washes. His work is lent great expressiveness and movement by the use of abbreviated shapes. Continuity is maintained by the use of white paper as the medium. This was not yet standard at the time, but offered the best surface for his subtle lighting effects.

The *Sleeping Female Nude with Putti and a Satyr* (ill. 112), dating from before 1630, Mena Marqués considers as an early example of Ribera's mature style, notable for its great technical freedom. It was a style he would preserve till the end.

If we compare the subjects of the drawings with those of the paintings, it is noticeable that religious subjects are relegated to the background. In his drawing, more prominently than in his paintings, the artist emerges as a keen observer and analyst of his time, whose attitude towards the world has already been compared to Galileo's. The *Study of bat and ears* (ill. 113) and the *Acrobats on the Rope* (ill. 110) belong in this context. In the bat study, both the animal and the ears are recorded with great accuracy, and the technique chosen, a red chalk drawing in which light and shadow effects are done by brush, is an excellent means to this end.

Pictures of saints among the drawings are limited to Ribera's principal cast of St. Bartholomew, St. Jerome and St. Sebastian, who are often shown simply as tormented people without special attributes. This circumstance has led some writers to conclude that Ribera was only interested in hermits and martyred saints because they offered an uninterrupted opportunity to devote himself to his real subject, the nude.

Although it is true that the private medium of drawing offers opportunities for working on an artist's real interests that are not possible with commissioned art, Ribera seems nonetheless a long way from an "art for art's sake" attitude or even a classical delight in anatomical studies. Such attitudes do not tally with the frequent scenes of graphic violence even in his secular depictions, like for example the horrifying *Execution Scene* from Haarlem (ill. 117).

The idea of considering and assessing form and content separately in Ribera's art seems likewise wholly out of place, with the drawing being praised as excellent and the gruesome content passed over as second-rate. Goya (1746–1828) has always been similarly misunderstood for the same reasons, when the public

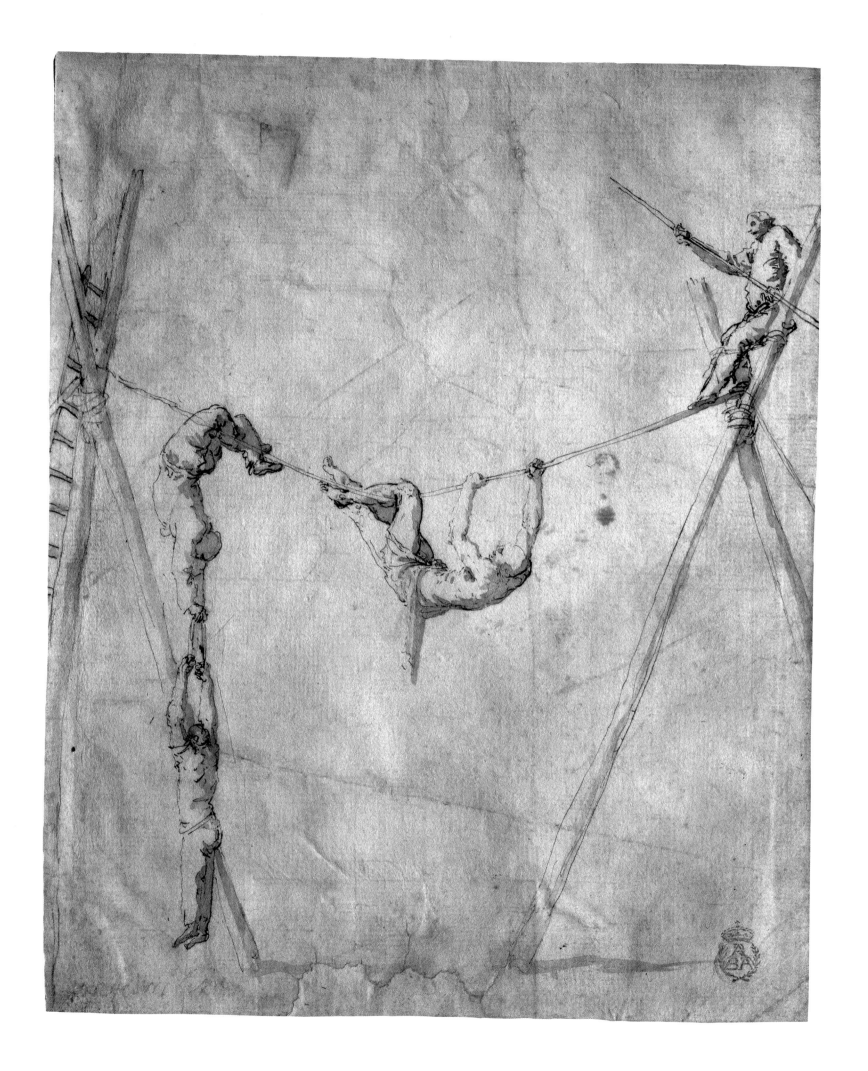

111 *Samson and Delilah*, c. 1626
Drawing, red chalk and black pencil on white paper,
28.2 x 40.4 cm
Museo Provincial de Bellas Artes, Córdoba

Though executed as a picture, this drawing is a study for
the painting of the same name which was destroyed in a
fire at the royal palace of Buen Retiro in 1808. It was
possibly intended to be shown to the king as a sample, so
that he could see what the planned composition would
contain. As only one other complete drawing of this sort
exists, and was intended for the same client, we can draw
no general conclusions about Ribera's working practices,
such as that he always made a complete preparatory
picture after many detailed studies.

112 *Sleeping Female Nude with Putti and a Satyr*,
1626–1630
Pen drawing with bistre wash on white paper,
17.5 x 25.9 cm
Fitzwilliam Museum, Cambridge

Though female nudes had many advocates in papal Rome,
they were frowned upon in Spanish-ruled territories.
We do nonetheless have a few Spanish examples, including
the famous *Rokeby Venus* by Velázquez. Ribera's
composition is based on a popular etching of the time by
Annibale Carracci. However, the nude figure itself could
be derived from a picture by Titian, which was sent from
Naples to Philip IV. The draftsmanship with short, self-
assured strokes and parallel hatchings is typical of Ribera's
style in the late 1620s.

whoops for joy at the subtle painting techniques used to depict scenes of murder and rape. Indeed, Aragon-born Goya, who was as brilliant a draftsman and graphic artist in the 18th century as Ribera was in his day, is probably the best point of comparison for scenes of violence. In their works both artists reacted to a particularly violent era resulting from radical social change, thereby giving us an opportunity to understand it better psychologically. Another aspect of Goya's art – that of social criticism, which bordered on caricature – calls to mind Ribera's *Master with his Squire* (ill. 116) of 1628.

Ribera's peculiar situation between cultures shows up in his drawing as well as his painting. Though the artist drew much in the Italian fashion, in terms of artistic form a very original combination of different models is discernible in his work. A few sheets in an academic style are outweighed by relatively numerous works that have the character of sketches of ideas or diary entries.

The printed graphics date mostly from a clearly defined period between 1620 and 1628, but to this day only 18 etchings by Ribera have been identified. Nevertheless, these few have made an important contribution to making the artist's work known.

According to Jonathan Brown, who has made a study of this part of Ribera's work for many years, the first of Ribera's known printed works date from around 1620. They are two depictions of saints, a *St. Sebastian*

and a *St. Bernadino of Siena*, and carry the hallmarks of a technical beginner. In chronological order, the following works were the figure of a poet, a *Pietá*, a *St. Peter Penitent* and two versions of *St. Jerome with the Angel of the Apocalypse*. The latter three are clearly related to paintings by Ribera, and are signed by the artist and dated to 1621. In the following year, Ribera seems to have planned a textbook for artists on the lines of other Italian manuals of drawing, and produced three plates, each showing various versions of facial features. One plate has ears, another eyes and the third is a sheet of *Studies of Noses and Mouths* (ill. 114). A grotesque head (ill. 115) may have been intended for a similar purpose, once again underlining Ribera's interest in bizarre figures and marginalized people.

Three further etchings dating from 1624–1628 are considered by Brown to be the best of Ribera's printed works. They include two depictions of saints who are similarly important among the artist's paintings, namely a *Martyrdom of St. Bartholomew* (ill. 118) and a *St. Jerome* crouching on the floor absorbed in his reading. In addition, there is a reproduction of the painting of *Drunken Silenus* (ill. 120) in several variants. Of uncertain date though likewise from the 1620s is a depiction by Ribera of a cupid thrashing a satyr chained to a tree.

After 1630 only two more etchings were produced, both of them probably commissioned. They include two figures of angels for the bearings of the Marqués de

113 *Study of bat and ears*, c. 1622
Red gouache plus red chalk on white paper, 16 x 27.8 cm
Metropolitan Museum of Art, New York

The ear motif, supplemented by further examples, recurs on one of three etchings that Ribera intended to publish as a manual for artists. The Latin inscription *FULGET SEMPER VIRTUS* (Virtue always shines) suggests a symbolic construction, but what it is we do not know. The bat with outspread wings, a virtuoso exercise in drawing showing all anatomical details, has had a very positive interpretation since Renaissance times. Among other things, it was a reference to the virginity of Diana, and was used in conjunction with the figure of the goddess as a protective symbol of birth and the care of small children. It is also found in the city bearings of Valencia.

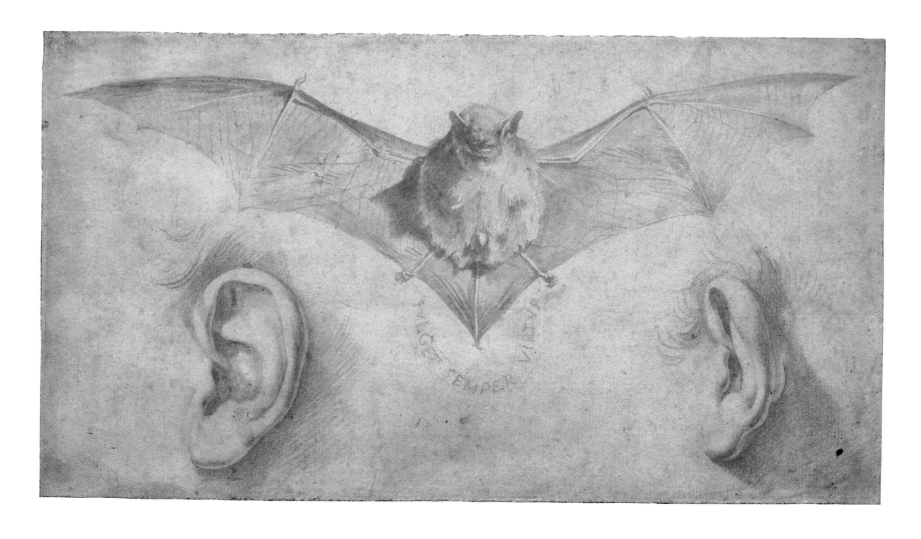

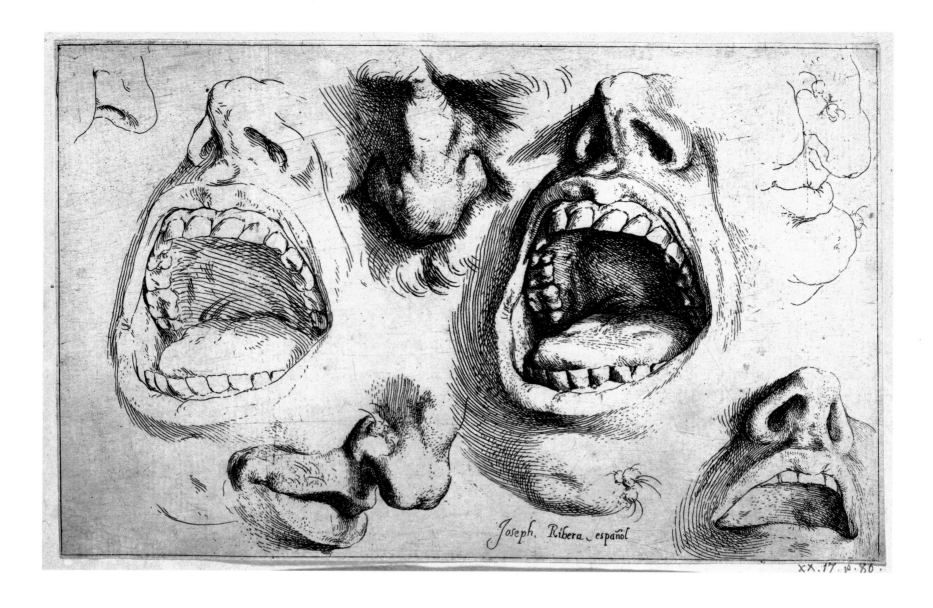

114 *Studies of noses and mouths*, c. 1622
Etching, 13.9 x 21.3 cm
Graphische Sammlung Albertina, Vienna

Of the three etchings that Ribera probably intended to go
in his manual of drawing, this one diverges most
noticeably from the usual studies. Instead of sober models,
the artist presents very individual interpretations of
selected details, so that even these fragments tell a personal
story. The mouth opened to scream recurs in Marsyas
as he is being flayed by Apollo (ills. 44, 46). A remarkable
feature is the obviously incorrect signature, which appears
on all known copies of the etching even though it was
probably etched into the plate under Ribera's supervision.
Though the *Joseph* instead of *Jusepe* is in itself unusual,
more so is the lack of the *de* between first and second
names.

Tarifa and a version of the equestrian portrait of *Don
Juan José de Austria* (ill. 119) dated 1648. In contrast
with the painting with its landscape background, the
latter features a prospect of the city of Naples and the
Spanish fleet sent to put down the Masaniello uprising.

Ribera's etchings reveal a quite astonishing technical
development by the artist. In just a few years, he was
transformed from a dilettante to a master, with his own
individudal style. In *St. Jerome*, who hears the trumpet
of the Last Judgement, we first find the stippling
typical of Ribera's etchings. This technique, plus the
numerous parallel hatchings instead of the normal
criss-cross technique, enables us to observe the change
to a light-filled style which took place earlier in the
printed graphics than in the paintings.

What then was the relationship between printed
graphics and painting? Seven of the known etchings are
in a general sense reproductions of Ribera's paintings.
When these and most of the other works were done in
the 1620s, Ribera was still at the beginning of his
career and, after the recent sudden recall of the Duke of
Osuna, temporarily deprived of his most important
patron. Everything indicates, therefore, that it was a
conscious choice to use printed graphics as a medium

to make his work better known outside Naples, thus
attracting the interest of new clients. The artist's intention also helps us to understand why his printed
graphic work dried up in the late 1620s just as he was
becoming known.

Yet it hardly does justice to Ribera's etchings to call
them just graphic reproductions. Unlike the works of
his Italian colleagues, his drawings for the proposed
manual have nothing of academic didacticism about
them. Despite their fragmentary nature, they represent
a wholly personal perspective. Moreover, in the printed
versions Ribera always endeavored to improve on his
paintings. This is quite evident from a comparison of
painted and etched versions in the case of the
Martyrdom of St. Bartholomew (ill. 118) and *Drunken
Silenus* (ill. 120).

The etchings provide proof that Ribera recognized
the importance of this new medium in his day, but like
El Greco (c. 1541–1614) continued to strive as an
artist and therefore did not derive much benefit from
his printed graphic work. It took an amazingly short
time for Ribera to master the techniques of etching,
but unlike Goya later (1736–1828) etching could
never fascinate him as a form of expression. Clearly, he

115 *Large grotesque head,* c. 1622
Etching, 21.7 x 14.5 cm
Graphische Sammlung Albertina, Vienna

Ribera's interest in this subject is borne out not just by a preliminary
study but also by a further etching for which he likewise did a
preparatory study. Over and above this another drawing survives,
though there the features of the physiognomy are not exaggerated in
this way. Certain details such as the warts recur in some of the face
fragments on the *Studies of noses and mouths* (ill. 114). Quite rightly,
it has been stressed that though Ribera shows us a grotesque head, as
with the portrait of *Magdalena Ventura* (ill. 49) his intention was to
analyze the phenomenon by depicting it. It is not a caricature, unlike
the famous drawings of grotesque heads by Leonardo.

116 *Master with his Squire,* 1628
Brush drawing in red gouache on white paper, 23 x 13.3 cm
J Paul Getty Museum, Los Angeles

The (for the time) unusual red watercolor was used by Ribera in
other drawings as well. The square lines presumably indicate that the
artist intended to transfer the motif into a larger painting. However,
it would probably only have been a marginal feature there, since the
sheet is cut on the left and the top. The humorous features of the
drawing have led to the supposition that Don Quixote and Sancho
Panza were intended. However, this hardly squares with the fact that
the first known illustrations of the famous work by Cervantes date
from the 18th century.

117 *Execution scene*, c. 1640
Pen drawing with bistre on yellowish paper,
13.2 x 26.8 cm
Teylers Museum, Haarlem

This drawing, which was attributed to Ribera's pupil
Salvator Rosa for a while, is now considered definitely to
be by Ribera, on the strength of the subject matter and the
drawing technique. The representation is among the most
brutal killing scenes the artist ever did, and is probably the
most conclusive answer to those who see his martyr figures
only as an interest in nude studies. It would be difficult to
imagine a painting of the same subject, and there is much
to suggest that Ribera was working out personal
impressions in this work. It should be borne in mind that
executions were deliberately carried out in public at the
time, as a more effective form of deterrence. From a
modern point of view, it appears scarcely comprehensible
that the perpetrators of serious offenses were also tortured
beforehand, not out of revenge but to spare them other
torments in hell.

118 (facing page)
Martyrdom of St. Bartholomew, 1624
Etching, 324 x 239 cm
Gabinetto dei Disegni e delle Stampe, Museo di
Capodimonte, Naples

This etching depicts a subject that Ribera had already
treated several times in paintings, the first being among
the pictures for the Duke of Osuna (ill. 28). Yet in its
gruesomeness the printed version surpasses all the other
versions. In the appended inscription, Ribera dedicated
the picture to the Viceroy of Sicily, perhaps in the hope
of gaining his patronage. Unfortunately, Prince Philibert
of Savoy died in the year it was produced.

perceived it only as a means to an end. Yet a graphic
artist as passionate as Rembrandt regarded Ribera's
work highly.

Even though the printed graphics brought Ribera
little tangible success at the time, they were of decisive
importance in establishing his reputation. The original
printing plate for *Drunken Silenus* was sold in 1650, in
other words while the artist was still alive. His various
etchings were later bundled together as a collection for
commercial distribution. Unfortunately they were
updated in a rather cavalier way that took little account
of the artist's original intentions. Thus a later version of
his most successful picture, *St. Jerome with the Angel of
the Apocalypse*, dispensed with the subsidiary figure,
and in the equestrian portrait of *Don Juan José de
Austria* (ill. 119), the portrait of the young viceroy was
swapped for one of Charles II.

C.46C

Dedico mis obras y esta estampa al Sereniss.mo Principe Philiberto mi señor
en Napoles año 1624   Iusepe de Riuera spañol

119 (facing page)
Don Juan José de Austria, 1648
Etching, 35 x 27 cm
Istituto Nazionale per la Grafica, Rome

We know of only two etchings by Ribera from the post-1628 period.
Quite clearly, the circumstances of the Masaniello uprising forced
him to return to the medium of etching, which was less interesting
as a form of artistic expression than as a means to reach a larger
public. The fact that here, in contrast to the painting (ill. 68), a
wealth of additional historical information is shown indicates that
the etching was intended to popularize the military success of Don
Juan José de Austria. Thus the background shows, a complete city
prospect, together with the Spanish fleet anchored in the harbor in
support of the viceroy, instead of the symbolic reference to the events
in Naples by means of a depiction of the Castel Sant' Elmo.

120 *Drunken Silenus*, 1628
Etching, 27.2 x 35 cm
Graphische Sammlung, Bayerische Staatsbibliothek, Munich

The improvements in this etching compared with the painting
completed two years earlier (ill. 87) show clearly that, though Ribera
generally refers back to his painted works, he does not simply
reproduce it. In this case, the background is completely revamped,
with the landscape and sky occupying more space. The lateral figures
in front of this foil are changed, and the donkey, which seems to be
mocking Silenus, is more effective against a light background.
The copper plate with Ribera's etching passed into the hands of a
Roman publisher in 1650, suggesting that the artist was forced
to sell it because of financial problems. In 1738 it was acquired by
the Calcografia Nazionale in Rome, which in 1933/34 issued
another series of reprints on modern paper.

CHRONOLOGY

1591   February 17: baptism of Joan Josep Ribera in Játiva. The name and spelling vary in later years according to the origin of the document. Ribera himself signs most of his pictures Jusepe de Ribera. His father is a cobbler.

1609/10   Philip III expels the Moriscos from Spain, causing an economic crisis in the Mediterranean region and probably also prompting Ribera's move to Italy.

1611   June 11: Ribera receives a payment for his picture of *St. Martin* (now lost) for a parish church in Parma.

1613   Ribera becomes a member of the Accademia di San Luca in Rome. The artist paints the *Allegories of the Five Senses*, in which he adopts a Caravaggesque chiaroscuro style.

1615/16   Ribera lives in the Via Margutta in Rome with his brother Juan and other Spanish nationals in a house belonging to a Fleming.

1616   Ribera leaves Rome for Naples, perhaps to escape his creditors, and marries Caterina Azzolino y India, the daughter of the distinguished Sicilian painter Giovanni Bernardino Azzolino.

1616–1618   Ribera paints a series of important paintings for the Duke of Osuna, which reveal the influence of Reni's classical style.

1618   The Thirty Years' War begins with the Defenestration of Prague. The Spanish war with the Dutch flares up again in 1621, and from then until the Treaty of the Pyrenees with France in 1659 Spain is involved in military conflict.

c. 1620   Physician Giulio Mancini writes the first biographical notes for Ribera in his *Considerazioni sulla Pittura*.

1620–1628   Ribera's most fruitful period for graphics, no doubt intended to boost his reputation and to gain new clients.

1623   Diego Velázquez appointed court painter in Madrid on the strength of his painting of the *The Water Seller of Seville* and similar works, which bear affinities with Ribera's *Allegories of the Five Senses*.

1625   Ribera is visited by the Spanish art writer Jusepe Martínez, who asks him why he doesn't return to the Iberian peninsula.

1626   January 29: Ribera is admitted to the Order of Christ in a ceremony at St. Peter's in Rome, which is an extraordinary recognition of his talent.

1630   Velázquez visits Naples and probably also visits Ribera.

1631   Ribera paints the portrait of *Magdalena Ventura* for the Duke of Alcalá, in office as viceroy of Naples from 1629 to 1631, and sets out his "art theory" in it.

1632   Ribera paints *Jacob and Laban's Flock*, the first picture in a new light-imbued period of his work, which also shows the influence of the Rome-based neo-Venetian style. A survey of university teachers' opinions of nudes in paintings, published in Madrid indicates a tightening of censorship in art within an Inquisition-style framework.

1633   During the pontificate of Urban VIII, Galileo Galilei is forced by the Inquisition to retract his declared belief in the Copernican theory of a planetary system revolving round the Sun.

1635   Ribera delivers five pictures for the burial chapel in Salamanca of the Count of Monterrey, viceroy of Naples 1631–1637. The architectural and sculptural work is the responsibility of Cosimo Fanzago, who, along with Lanfranco, is one of the closest artistic associates of Ribera in Naples.

From 1637 Sundry works for the decoration of the Certosa di San Martino in Naples. The final works are only completed in 1651.

1638 The Spanish Inquisition confirms Ribera's origin in Játiva.

1641 After the sudden death of Domenichino in Naples, Ribera is among those suspected of murder. Nonetheless, he is commissioned to paint an altar painting for Domenichino's unfinished Cappella del Tesoro di San Gennaro in Naples Cathedral.

c. 1644 Ribera falls seriously ill, which restricts his work considerably until 1651. His large workshop takes over part of the work during the period. Ribera's eldest daughter Margarita marries Giovanni Leonardo Sersale, judge of the Tribunale della Vicaria, which means a major social rise for the family for a short while.

1647/48 Ribera takes refuge in the viceregal palace during the Masaniello uprising. He paints an equestrian picture of *Don Juan José de Austria*, the victor over the rebels, and also makes an etching of the painting.

1649 In the posthumously published art treatise by Francisco Pacheco *Arte de la Pintura*, Ribera is compared with Caravaggio and Velázquez.

1652 September 3: Ribera dies in dire financial straits in Mergellina near Naples, where he had rented a house only the previous July. After his death, the artist exercises a powerful influence on painters everywhere in Europe.

1675 In his treatise *Teutsche Academie* Joachim von Sandrart passes judgment on Ribera's pictures of violence, thus establishing a long-term image of the artist.

1838–1848 Ribera's pictures are greeted with especial interest in the Spanish gallery established in Paris by the citizen king Louis-Philippe because they are considered particularly typical for the national school of Spain.

1908 August L. Mayer publishes a first critical catalog of Ribera's works in Leipzig.

GLOSSARY

Academy (Lat. *academia*, Gk. *akademia*), body, institution, or society for the promotion of artistic or academic study and education. The most important Renaissance academies were established in Milan and Florence on the basis of schools of Antiquity. The idea of the academy spread throughout Europe during the period of absolutism. The main models are the Académie Française, founded in 1635, and the Académie Royale de Peinture et de Sculpture, founded in 1648. The visual arts academy in Venice was not founded until 1754. The term "academy" is believed to refer to a garden near Athens that was dedicated to the Attic hero Academus and contained facilities for gymnastic training. A favorite spot of Plato, he names the school of philosophy that he established in 387 B.C. after it.

Adoration of the Shepherds A scene based on St. Luke's Gospel, chapter 2. After the birth of Christ, three shepherds were told to leave their flocks and go to the manger. A very popular subject in paintings in the 15th–17th centuries.

Agnes, St. Roman martyr † c. 305 A.D. Documented 354, when a church was built over her grave. Fifth-century tradition records her as a girl of 13 who had her throat cut rather than lose her virginity. The Golden Legend tells her story in detail: she was a devout Christian who was lusted after by the prefect's son and stripped naked in public by his father as a punishment for not giving in. In the event, her hair grew to cover her.

allegory (Gk. *allegorein*, "express differently") The representation of abstract concepts by means of symbols or concrete stories or scenes.

Amos The earliest of the twelve minor prophets, dating from c. 8th B.C. One of the shorter books in the Old Testament.

Apelles (fl. 330 B.C.) Greek painter and court painter of Alexander the Great. Though none of his paintings has survived, Renaissance painters tried to reconstruct them from literary descriptions.

Apollo Greek god, the son of Zeus and Leto, twin of Diana. He appears as many other things beside the god of the arts, e.g. the god of light and the sun. He also represented masculine beauty.

apostle (Gk. *apostolos*, "messenger") One of the twelve disciples of Jesus, who had all been selected by him personally. Later St. Paul was also called an apostle, although he had not met Jesus personally.

attribute (Lat. *attributum*, "added") An object shown with a saint in a picture as a means of identification for the believer. For example, St. Jerome often has a lion, because he once extracted a thorn from a lion's paw.

Bacchus (Dionysius) The god of wine, the son of Jupiter (Zeus) and Semele. Silenus was his foster-father.

Bamboccianti From Italian *bamboccio* (clumsy fellow, squirt). Name of a group of 17th-century Dutch artists in Italy who painted scenes of street life. Named for their leader Pieter van Laer (pre-1599–after 1642), who was deformed.

Baroque A period in European art between the end of Mannerism (c. 1590) and Rococo (c. 1725). The style originated in Rome, and is associated with the Catholic Counter-Reformation. It therefore developed principally in Catholic countries. The most obvious characteristics are exuberance and movement, sometimes verging on the florid and excessive.

Bartholomew, St. One of the apostles. Nothing certain is known about his life or death, but he is said to have preached in India and Armenia, where he was flayed alive and then beheaded, traditionally at Derbend on the Caspian Sea.

bistre Brown lampblack made from the soot of burnt beechwood. Known since the 14th century, it was most famously used by Rembrandt.

bodegón (Sp. "inn, tavern", pl. *bodegones*) Spanish picture genre greatly popular in 17th century, combining still lifes and genre scenes of lower class life. The word comes from *bodega*, an inn room where simple people had meals. The genre developed from Flemish kitchen scenes, and in Spain was most popular in Seville and Toledo. In his early period, Velázquez was an enthusiastic practitioner. The genre helped Spanish art to cast off Mannerism and develop its naturalistic tendencies. Eventually the term came to mean just a still life.

Bruno, St. (11th century) Founder of the Carthusian Order, educated at Rheims and Cologne, though his last years were spent in Italy. A friend of Roger Guiscard, brother of swashbuckling Robert Guiscard, first Norman duke of Sicily.

Calvary The site of the Crucifixion, and by extension a picture of Christ on the Cross, raised on three steps, usually with Mary and John on either side.

Cano, Alonso (1601–67) Granada-born Spanish sculptor, painter, architect and priest who worked in Seville (where he trained under Pacheco with Velázquez) and Madrid. Apart from the *Immaculate Conception* statue, his masterpiece is the Baroque facade of Granada Cathedral. In 1644, he was arrested on suspicion of murdering his second wife, but was later freed.

Capuchins Originally a branch of the Franciscan friars, founded by Matteo di Bassi in 1520, but became independent in 1619. The name comes from the *capuche* (pointed hood) of their brown habits.

Caravaggesque In the style of Caravaggio (1571–1610), who was born near Milan (Lombardy). His work in the French church in Rome was his first big commission, but was initially rejected because it breached "decorum". In his style, he disavowed polite idealism in favor of a vivid realism dramatized by strong chiaroscuro effects, simplicity of subject and great everyday detail. His life was violent and turbulent, but he died of natural causes (fever) in a tavern.

Carthusian Order Founded by St. Bruno in the Chartreuse district of France in 1084. A Carthusian establishment is called a Certosa in Italy and a Charterhouse in England. The order cultivated the hermit life.

chiaroscuro A painting technique based on a strong (but balanced) contrast between pronounced light and dark areas, in order to create an impression of depth.

Church State (*Patrimonium Petri*) The sovereign state in central Italy controlled by the papacy. Created in the 8th century by donations from kings, it was extended by conquest until by the 16th century it comprised virtually all of central Italy. Occupied by Italy in 1870, papal sovereignty was henceforth reduced to the Vatican City.

classical painting Used in the context of this book to refer to the style of Renaissance classicism, i.e. the painters who took the art of antiquity as inspiration. The subject matter is idealized. Guido Reni's classical style was based both on classical antiquity and the art of Raphael.

confessionalization A new term propounded by historians Wolfgang Reinhard and Heinz Schilling to cover all theological reform movements of the 16th and 17th centuries, including the Reformation, Catholic reform and the Counter Reformation. This new concept no longer regards the Catholic Reformation as a reactionary response to the reform movement of Martin Luther (1483–1546) and John Calvin (1509–1564), but rather as an integral component of the transformation processes that led to the establishment of a modern democratic and industrial society.

Counter-Reformation The traditional term for the Catholic Church's reorganization in response to the Reformation, in an attempt to stop it spreading. It is usually dated from the decisions taken at the Council of Trent (1545–63). Its principal results were a century of bloody religious wars, the entrenchment of the Inquisition in other countries besides Spain and the rise of the Jesuits as an educational and missionary force.

decoro The principal of ethical and moral decorum included in the picture decree of the Council of Trent and based on a concept set out by the Roman architect Vitruvius (born c. 84 B.C.) It covers not only the relationship between pictorial realization and subject matter but also the manner and location of public display.

Democritus (c. 460–361 B.C.) A Greek philosopher and speculative scientist who made a major contribution to metaphysics, based on an atomic theory of the universe. He traveled over most of Europe and the known parts of Asia and Africa in quest of knowledge, and returned home in the greatest poverty. He continually laughed at the follies and vanities of mankind.

van Dyck, Anthony (1599–1641) Flemish painter, initially Rubens' assistant. Spent six years in Italy in the 1620s, but plague drove him back to Flanders. He spent most of the last years of his life in England painting portraits, but felt very insecure there because of the political problems of Charles I, his patron. His English portraits were influential for English painters for a long time after his death.

Earthly Trinity The Holy Family as an earthly unit corresponding to the heavenly trinity of God the Father, Son and Holy Ghost. The trinities are sometimes found together in one picture in a type called the Two Trinities.

El Greco (1541–1614) Cretan-born painter Domenikos Theotokopoulos, who was the first great artist of the Spanish school. Relatively little is known of his works in the Byzantine manner before he emigrated to Italy c. 1567. Ten years later he moved to Toledo, where he remained until he died. His paintings are always signed in Greek script with his real name.

etching A print made from a drawing etched on a metal plate with the help of a needle and a mordant (acid). The technique was developed in the early 16th century by Daniel Hopfer. The earliest plates were iron, but results soon proved much more satisfactory with copper and then steel.

five senses Sight, hearing, smell, taste and touch. The subject was especially popular in art in the Netherlands from the late 16th to mid-17th centuries. Initially they were shown as personifications, but then developed into everyday activities in realistic settings. Popular scenes include women in front of mirrors (sight), peasants smoking (taste) and music-making (hearing). Still lifes were sometimes used, e.g. flowers for the sense of smell.

genre painting A painting showing a scene of everyday life, especially the inside of a house or a village scene.

glory A halo or aura of light around the figure of a saint, which during the Counter-Reformation could take the form of separate light rays. In the case of God the Father, Christ, the Holy Spirit and the Virgin, the aura generally envelopes the whole body. A halo is just a circle behind or above the head, sometimes called a nimbus.

Golden Legend (*Legenda Aurea*) A compilation of legends, traditions and ancient writings about the lives of the saints written in the mid-13th century by Jacobus de Voragine. First published in English by Caxton in 1483. It was one of the most important sources of iconography for medieval and early Renaissance art.

gouache Water-soluble paint, though unlike water colors opaque rather than transparent, as a result of chalk being added. The pigments are mixed with a binder (gum arabic or dextrin) and opaque white, which produces a matt chalky appearance. Gouache was particularly used for miniature portraits from the 15th century, as the colors got brighter on drying, and also because sculptural effects could be obtained.

graphics All the various processes by which prints are produced. Also includes drawings in general, as part of the process, engravings, etchings etc.

humanism An intellectual movement born in Italy in the mid-14th century, devoted to rediscovering and disseminating Greek and Latin languages and literature. A humanistic education was intended to combine a thorough knowledge of these with more general modern empirical knowledge of the real world and nature. In contrast with medieval philosophy, where God was the source of all knowledge, the humanists focused on man's own experience of the world.

iconography The systematization of visual subject matter, meaning and symbolism so that viewers can understand pictures. The Virgin's iconography, for example, includes such things as the color of her cloak, her attributes, her position in relation to other figures in the pictures, etc. In terms of saints, iconography includes their attributes and the way they are presented (e.g. as hermits or philosophers, dead or alive, etc.) in a religious context.

Immaculate Conception The dogma that Mary was conceived virginally, like Christ, and was therefore free of original sin. The belief is longstanding in the eastern Church, but did not become popular in the west until the 16th century. The Spanish monarchs made a crusade of the issue, and it was finally made dogma in 1854.

Inquisition An institution originally introduced by Pope Gregory IX in 1233 to suppress the Cathar heresy, and subsequently the Templars. It became particularly active in Spain in the late 15th century under Torquemada as an instrument for killing, expelling or forcibly converting Jews, heretics and Arabs following the re-conquest. Following the Council of Trent, its role became more fundamental as a means of political and religious control in all Catholic countries. It is now renamed and part of the Holy Office in Rome.

Ixion A king of Thessaly who treacherously murdered his father-in-law Deioneus, as a result of which he was shunned by his fellow princes. Jupiter had compassion on him and took him off to heaven. Instead of being grateful, Ixion seduced Jupiter's wife Juno. Accordingly, Jupiter had him tied to a wheel in hell that whirled in perpetual motion.

Jacob An Old Testament patriarch, son of Isaac and Rebecca, younger brother of Esau. Rebecca persuaded Isaac to send Jacob to her brother Laban to find himself a bride. On the way, at Bethel, 12 miles from Jerusalem, Jacob lay down to sleep, with his head on a stone, and dreamt of a ladder rising to heaven. At the top stood God, promising that the land on which he lay would be his and his children's, the Promised Land. When he reached Laban's land, Jacob fell in love with Laban's daughter Rachel. Thereafter Laban proceeded to cheat Jacob into remaining there as a servant for 20 years, using various tricks involving Laban's sheep.

Januarius, St. (St. Gennaro) Bishop of Benevento, martyred somewhere near Naples c. 305. The most memorable feature of his cult is the liquefaction of the relic of his blood, which has taken place every year since 1389, though it did not happen when Naples elected a Communist mayor!

Jerome, St. (c. 341–420) Doctor of the Church. Born in Dalmatia, he also traveled in Gaul and Italy, then Syria, where he became a hermit in the desert for five years. Highly educated, he knew Latin, Greek and Hebrew, and soon felt more at home in Constantinople. He translated the whole Bible into Latin, which is essentially the modern Vulgate. His concern was for accuracy of translation. Jerome's biting tongue and sarcastic wit made him many enemies. He finished his days as a monk in Bethlehem, where he was buried under the Church of the Nativity, though the body was later translated to Rome.

Joel A minor Old Testament prophet (c. 400 B.C.), with a very brief Book of his own notable for its vision of the end of the world.

landscape painting A painting in which the scenery itself is the subject. Generally consists of a foreground rather like a stage proscenium looking on to a distant background. Many medieval paintings had landscape features in the background, but it was not until the early 16th century that Albrecht Altdorfer painted the first landscapes in the modern sense. The classical landscapes of Lorrain and Poussin generally include architectural features reminiscent of classical antiquity.

lazzaroni Early 17th-century term for the lower classes in Naples, as a distinct social group.

Magdalene, Mary (1st century) The quintessential sinner who repents. She was a follower of Christ, who cured her of "seven devils". She was there at the Crucifixion, and on the morning of Easter Sunday. She was also identified with the sinner who anointed Christ's feet (St. Luke 7, 37). Her usual attribute is a pot of ointment.

Maria Aegyptiaca (St. Mary of Egypt, 5th century) Recorded in various ancient documents. According to the *Golden Legend*, she was an Egyptian girl who became a prostitute in Alexandria at 12, joined a pilgrimage to Jerusalem aged 29, had a vision there, and crossed the Jordan to become a hermit for another 47 years, naked after her clothes wore out and living off three loaves. A monk called Zozimus then met her, aged 76, and arranged for her to have communion, after which she died. A lion and Zozimus dug her grave.

Marsyas A celebrated Phrygian piper, son of Olympus. He was considered the inventor of the flute. He fell in love with the goddess Cybele, and traveled with her to Nyssa, where he challenged Apollo to a musical duel. It was agreed between them that the loser should be flayed alive. In the contest, the Muses had great difficulty in deciding who should be the winner, but finally chose Apollo. Marsyas's death at Apollo's hands was universally lamented by fauns, satyrs and dryads, and a Phrygian river was named for him.

Masaniello A leader of the popular uprising against the Spanish in Naples in 1647/48. He was murdered fairly early on.

Mater Dolorosa (Virgin of Sorrows) A term covering various different types of picture relating to the Virgin and the Crucifixion. The type here is that of the Mother supporting the body of her Son's dead body, grief stricken. If she were not grief-stricken but meditative, the picture would be a *Pietà*.

naturalism Any style of art or literature that tries to reproduce reality as experienced through the senser and as close to nature as possible, often with scientific precision.

oil painting Painting with paints containing oils (linseed, poppy, walnut) added in various ways as a binder. Though painters such as Bellini begin to use oil paints as an additional technique in the early 16th century, it was another 100 years before oil paints on canvas were used for the whole picture.

Ovid (43 B.C.–18 A.D.) Publius Ovidius Naso, author of the *Metamorphoses*, telling of the metamorphoses of Greek and Roman mythology. It is at the same time a description of human development from the primeval creation of the world to the imperial days of the Augustan era.

Pan In Greek mythology, the god of the woods and shepherds, the son of Hermes and a nymph, with cloven hoofs and horns. In the retinue of the god Dionysius (Bacchus), he leads the satyrs and waylays nymphs, one of whom, Syrinx ("pipe" in Greek), is turned into a reed as she flees from him. Pan uses the reed for his first panpipes. Pan's favorite abode is Arcadia.

paragone (Ital., "comparison") Term for the dispute concerning the supremacy in the arts, a popular theme in the Renaissance period, and widely reflected in theoretical writings on art.

Penitent Magdalene A type of picture showing Mary Magdalene, a very popular devotional figure in all centuries. See Magdalene.

Philip, St. Apostle mentioned in the Gospel of St. John. In art, his attributes are a cross, on which he may have died, and loaves of bread, due to a remark he made at the feeding of the 5,000.

picaresque A type of novel developed in Spain as a special genre of adventure novel recounting the memoirs of rogues, vagrants and adventurers. Mostly first-person narratives, the novels often include satire and social criticism. A major writer of such novels was Mateo Alemán (1547–c. 1614), whose most famous work was *Guzmán de Alfarache* (1599/1604).

picture decree In the final session of the Council of Trent in 1563, decisions were taken as to the invocation of saints, the veneration of relics and use of pictures. The decree permitted the religious use of pictures of Christ, Mary and the saints, stipulating that worshippers be instructed about intercessions and the invocation of the saints, the veneration of relics and the correct use of pictures. The decree also declared that pictures should always remind churchgoers about the mystery of the Redemption of Christ, depictions of saints should encourage imitation of virtuous behavior and they should be conducive to edification. The decree contains regulations for the iconography of religious art, which was to eschew all dishonest, ambiguous, immoral or even just disorderly or secular character.

pietà A meditative rather than a grief-stricken version of a Mater Dolorosa.

pince-nez A pair of spectacles kept in place by a spring, which grips the nose.

putto (Ital. *putto*, pl. *putti*, "boy") A small, naked cherub with or without wings. An invention of the early Italian Renaissance based on the child angels of Gothic art on the model of classical Cupids.

red chalk (sanguine) A chalk that contains iron oxide.

repoussoir A figure or object in the foreground of a picture (e.g. tree stump or architectural fragment) that enhances the sense of depth by pushing back the distant scene optically.

retable An elaborate carved or painted altarpiece behind the altar.

Roch, St. (c. 1350–1380) Born in Montpellier to a rich merchant family, he spent much of his short life as a pilgrim. In Piacenza he caught the plague, and was fed by a dog, but miraculously he cured others of it. He appears to have died in prison as a suspected spy. He is a patron of plague sufferers, and is shown as a pilgrim with a sore on his leg, or with a dog.

Roomer, Gaspar An Antwerp-born merchant who was the richest foreigner in Naples in Ribera's day, and owned 1,500 paintings at his death. He played a large part in familiarizing Italian artists with northern European art.

Rubens, Peter Paul (1577–1640) Flemish painter and diplomat who knew six languages fluently. Born a Calvinist, he became a devout Catholic. His style developed in Italy from 1600, where he worked mainly in Genoa and Rome. In 1609 he returned to Antwerp and instantly became successful, being appointed court painter to the Spanish viceroy. Demand for his work was huge, but he supplied it by running a very efficient workshop. He worked for the royal families of France, England and Spain, doing over a hundred mythological pictures for the latter, most of which were destroyed in 1710 during the War of the Spanish Succession.

Sebastian, St. († c. 300) A Roman Christian martyred during the Diocletian persecutions, and one of the Fourteen Holy Helpers, among whom he was a plague specialist. He was buried under the Appian Way near the church named for him. The story of his being shot to death with arrows derives from a dubious 5th-century source, but nonetheless proved to be was an extremely popular subject in 15th-century art.

siglo de oro The Golden Age, describing a period in Spanish literature from 1520–1680.

Silenus A demi-god who was the nurse, preceptor and attendant of the god Bacchus. He was supposedly the son of Pan. He is generally represented as a fat, jolly old man, riding on a donkey and always intoxicated.

Spanish School 19th-century term for 16th/17th-century painting. The school was distinguished by its naturalistic style and unconventional saints. The French king Louis Philippe (1773–1850) acquired 450 paintings of Spanish masters and opened a special gallery in the Louvre in 1838 to house them. The pictures made a great impression on the Parisian art world. The principal names are Ribera, Zurbarán (1598–1664) and Velázquez.

still life A picture of lifeless objects artistically arranged, such as flowers, fruit, books, vessels and dead game. The genre first appeared in the late 14th century, and reached a peak in 17th-century Dutch painting. Cf. *bodegón*.

tenebrism (Ital. *tenebroso*, "obscure") A term describing predominantly dark tonality in painting, adopted by followers of Caravaggio (1573–1610), though they themselves did not use the term.

Titian (c. 1485–1576) A pupil of Bellini, and the greatest painter of the Venetian school. A close colleague of Giorgione, many of whose pictures he had to finish after the latter's premature death. The greatest patron of his later career was Philip II of Spain, for whom he did a series of seven erotic mythological subjects.

Tityus A giant, who covered nine acres when stretched out. He threatened violence to Latona, the daughter of a Titan (and amour of Jupiter), at which she called in her sons. They killed Tityus with their arrows. He was sent to hell, where a serpent continually devoured his liver, or, in another tradition, vultures perpetually gnawed his entrails.

translation The removal of a saint from earth to heaven, originally without death, though later it simply meant the death of the saint.

Trent, Council of (1545–1563) A series of meetings by the Catholic monarchs and the Church to formalize Church reform and stop the spread of the Reformation. Its principal effect was to institutionalize religious intolerance and promote religious warfare. The adjective is Tridentine.

veduta (Ital. *veduta*, pl. *vedute*, "view") A topographically accurate drawing of a landscape or city.

viceroy A high-ranking courtier appointed to rule a foreign possession that was technically a kingdom. Naples and Sicily were both kingdoms and viceroyalties of Spain.

SELECTED BIBLIOGRAPHY

Jusepe de Ribera, Prints and Drawings, Art Museum, Princeton University 1973

Jusepe de Ribera, *Lo Spagnoletto, 1591–1652*, Kimbell Art Museum, Fort Worth, Washington University Press 1982

Painting in Naples, 1606–1705. From Caravaggio to Giordano, Royal Academy of Arts, London 1982

Ribera 1591–1652, Museo del Prado, Madrid 1992

Jonathan Brown: *Images and Ideas in 17th Century Spanish Painting*, Princeton 1978

Sven Externbrink and Michael Scholz-Hänsel: "Ribera und die 'Gegenreformation' in Süditalien. Vom Nutzen der neuen historischen Paradigmata Konfessionalisierung und Sozialdisziplinierung für die Kunstgeschichte," in: *Kritische Berichte*, Vol. 24, Marburg 1996, issue 3, pp. 20–36

Craig Felton: *Jusepe de Ribera. A Catalogue Raisonné*, 2 vols., diss. University of Pittsburgh 1971

Spanische Kunstgeschichte. *Eine Einführung*, 2 vols. ed. Sylvaine Hänsel and Henrik Karge, Berlin 1992, vol. 2: Von der Renaissance bis heute

Francis Haskell: *Patrons and Painters: A Study in the Relations between Italian Art and Society in the Age of the Baroque*, London 1980

Carl Justi: *Diego Velazquez und sein Jahrhundert*, Bonn 1903

Gérard Labrot: *Collections of Paintings in Naples 1600–1780*, Munich 1992

August L Mayer: *Jusepe de Ribera, Lo Spagnoletto*, Leipzig 1908

Francisco Pacheco: *El Arte de la Pintura*, ed. Bonaventura Bassegoda i Hugas, Madrid 1990

Alfonso E. Pérez Sánchez and Nicola Spinosa: *L'Opera completa di Jusepe de Ribera*, Milan 1987

Alfonso E. Pérez Sánchez: *Ribera*, Madrid 1994

Jean-Michel Sallmann: *Naples et ses saints à l'âge baroque (1540–1750)*, Paris 1994

Suzanne Stratton: *La Inmaculada Concepción en el Arte Español*, Madrid 1988

Werner Weisbach: *Der Barock als Kunst der Gegenreformation*, Berlin 1921

PICTURE CREDITS

The publisher thanks the following museums, collectors, librarians and photographers who gave permission for reproduction:

© Allen Memorial Art Museum, Oberlin College, Oberlin, Ohio – R. T. Miller, Jr. Fund, 1955 (103); © Archiv für Kunst und Geschichte, Berlin (88 left); © Archivi Alinari, Florence (105, 117); © Artothek, Peissenberg – photo: Bayer/Mitko (14), Blauel/Gnamm (13), Schiller (88 right); © Bayerische Staatsbibliothek, Munich (68); © Bridgeman Art Library, London (21); © Serge Dominigie/Marco Rabatti, Florence (42/43); © By kind permission of the Earl of Pembroke and the Trustees of Wilton House Trust, Salisbury/Wilts (63); © Fitzwilliam Museum, Cambridge/England (126 below); © Fundación Banco Santander Central Hispano, Madrid (46); © Galleria Colonna, Rome – photo: Arte Fotografica, Rome (19); © Galleria Corsini, Rome [inv. no. 233] (53); © The J. Paul Getty Museum, Los Angeles (82 below, 129 right); © Graphische Sammlung Albertina, Vienna (128, 129 left); © Great Art Inc., Tortola, Virgin Islands (17); © Map Division/New York Public Library – Astor, Lennox and Tilden Foundations, New York (67); © Alger H. Meadows Collection, Meadows Museum, Southern Methodist University, Dallas, Texas [acc. no. 77.07] (30); © Metropolitan Museum of Art, Rogers Fund, 1972 (1972.77) photo; © 1984 Metropolitan Museum of Art – photo: Bob Hanson (127); © Musée Bonnat, Bayonne (9); © Musée des Beaux-Arts, Rouen – photo: Didier Tragin/Catherine Lancien (11); © Musée Fabre, Montpellier – photo: Frédéric Jaulmes – Reproduction interdite (85); © Musée Royaux des Beaux-Arts de Belgique, Brussels – photo: Cussac (54 above, 56); © Museo Nacional del Prado, Madrid (51, 52, 72, 86, 93, 101); © Museo Provincial de Bellas Artes, Córdoba – photo: Michael Zapke (126 above); © Museo Thyssen-Bornemisza, Madrid (45); © Museu Nacional d'Art de Catalunya, Barcelona – photo: Calveras, Mérida, Sagristà (39); © Museum of Fine Arts of Alava, Vitoria – photographic archives (74); © Museum of the Royal Academy of Fine Arts of San Fernando, Madrid (76); © 1999 Board of Trustees, National Gallery of Art, Washington – gift of the 50th Anniversary Gift Committee (41); © Norton Simon Foundation, Pasadena, CA (7); © Oronoz, Madrid (26, 33, 34, 35, 47, 49, 59, 65, 77 left, 80 top, 82 top, 124); © Österreichische Nationalbibliothek, Vienna – Bildarchiv (18); © Patrimonio Nacional, Madrid (79); © Luciano Pedicini/Archivio dell'Arte, Napoli (12, 15, 20, 25, 66, 70, 71, 77 right, 104, 106, 107, 110, 111, 115, 119, 122, 131); © Pinacoteca Nazionale, Bologna (37); © SCALA group SpA, Antella/Florence (8, 23, 27 left, 55, 57, 73, 75, 83, 87, 89, 91, 92, 97, 100, 114, 121, 123); © Teylers Museum, Haarlem [inv. no. E20] (130); © Victoria and Albert Picture Library, London (29); © Wadsworth Atheneum, Hartford – Ella Gallup Sumner and Mary Catlin Sumner Collection Fund, Hartford/Connecticut (27 right); © Gerald Zugmann, Vienna (24).